HI YA!!

Introduction to Music Education

SECOND EDITION

Introduction to Music Education

CHARLES R. HOFFER
University of Florida

Wadsworth Publishing Company

Belmont, California • A Division of Wadsworth, Inc.

Music Education Editor: Suzanna Brabant

Editorial Assistant: Dana Lipsky

Production Editor: Donna Linden

Managing Designer: Carolyn Deacy

Print Buyer: Barbara Britton

Permissions Editor: Jeanne Bosschart

Designer: Wendy Calmenson

Copy Editor: Rebecca Magee

Cover Designer: William Reuter

Cover Photographs: Nita Winter

Compositor: G&S Typesetters, Inc., Austin, Texas

Printer: Fairfield Graphics, Fairfield, Pennsylvania

Photo Credits: p. 4: Courtesy Wichita Symphony Orchestra, Wichita, Kansas. Pp. 3, 15, 35, 67, 93, 115, 135: Courtesy of Music Educators National Conference, Reston, Virginia. P. 43: © Peter Gridley and Courtesy of Music Educators National Conference, Reston, Virginia. Pp. 55, 79: Courtesy of Charles R. Hoffer.

This book is printed on
acid-free recycled paper.

Printed in the United States of America

4   5   6   7   8   9   10—97   96   95

Library of Congress Cataloging-in-Publication Data

Hoffer, Charles R.
  Introduction to music education / Charles R. Hoffer. — 2nd ed.
      p.   cm.
  Includes bibliographical references and index.
  ISBN 0-534-19452-4
  1. School music—Instruction and study.   I. Title.
MT1.H723   1992
780'.7—dc20   92-18543

To

Andrew Allan Hoffer
Kendall Renee Hoffer
Lucas Latham Teater
Kevin Robert Teater

May the joy of music fill their lives.

CONTENTS

PREFACE

M*any* colleges and universities have a course that introduces prospective school music teachers to the profession of music education. This course seeks to get the future teachers thinking about music teaching. It also encourages the students to examine themselves in terms of becoming music teachers. In addition, it provides an overview of the field, including some of its opportunities and its challenges. As the title implies, the course precedes the methods courses in which the students learn techniques for teaching various aspects of music. *Introduction to Music Education,* Second edition, seeks to provide students and instructors with information and activities to help the course fulfill these goals.

The second edition of *Introduction to Music Education* has been extensively revised. First, its content has been brought up to date. Second, this edition has been shortened quite a bit. Many introductory courses meet only once or twice each week. Therefore, the amount of material that can be covered is limited. Third, the overlap of material with *Teaching Music in the Secondary Schools,* Fourth edition, has been greatly reduced. Only a limited amount of the content is similar, mainly those portions that usually merit a second look anyway. Fourth, the order in which topics are presented has been greatly changed. In general, it moves from the nature of teaching and of teachers to the music education profession.

I would like to thank the many persons who encouraged and enlightened me in my efforts to be a teacher and a writer. Citing a few names here would not be fair to the many who would not be mentioned. I can only thank them as a group and hope that this is adequate. I do wish to thank the following persons for their reviews of the manuscript: Barbara Bennett, Baylor University; Linda Crowe, Southeast Missouri State University; Hildegard Froehlich, University of North Texas; Russell A. Hammar, Kalamazoo College; Patricia Hughes, University of Northern Iowa; William D. Hughes, Florida State University; Gary Johnston,

xiii

Northern Kentucky University; Gary M. Martin, University of Oregon; Eleanor Meurer, Indiana State University; Samuel D. Miller, University of Houston; Mary Ann Norton, Boston University; James Scholten, Ohio University; Ruth Shaw, East Carolina University; Eugenia Sinor, Indiana University; and Leona Frances Woskowiak, Millersville University.

Introduction to Music Education

CHAPTER 1

The Importance of Teaching Music

It all begins here. It has to. Unless music has value for people, especially young people, then the whole idea of music education is in deep trouble. If music makes little or no difference in the lives of people, there is little point in spending time and effort educating them in it. Yes, music education begins with a clear understanding of why it is important for people and for the quality of their lives.

For present and future music teachers there is an additional reason why music education begins with the importance of teaching and learning music. The reasons why music is important have a lot to say about what and how music should be taught. For example, if music is seen as a nice extracurricular activity with little educational content, then music teachers will not be concerned about what the students learn. On the other hand, if music is seen as something vital in the education of every student, then music teachers will take actions to ensure that every student learns basic music skills and knowledge. The reasons for music in the schools not only provide the starting place, they also point the direction for music educators.

This introduction to music education, then, begins at the beginning by digging into the reasons for music in the schools.

The picture on page 4 makes its point very effectively: Life without music would be pretty bleak and dreary. People would not physically die if they didn't

have music, but a little of the quality of their lives would be missing. Psychologically they would be worse off, and their spirits would be diminished and dulled. Music makes a difference in people's lives.

The message on the picture, "Imagine the world without music," also applies to societies and civilizations. Without music the quality of life in America would be less than it is now. It would lack some of its vitality and vigor. The nation would be poorer, not only economically, but also in how its citizens act and feel.

Music and the other arts represent an important difference between existing and living. Animals exist in the sense that they manage to survive; that's their objective in existing. Humans live; they attempt to make life interesting, rewarding, and satisfying. Humans are not content merely to get by, to survive. Music, painting, and dance enrich life and bring to it their special meanings by providing an avenue for expression. People admire the shifting surf, the color of a sky at sunset, the beauty of a flower. They also create objects that they can contemplate and with which they can enrich their lives. For example, although a rather large cardboard box could serve as a nightstand by your bed (and it would cost nothing), you really would rather have a wooden table or stand with a little grace and beauty. This compulsion of humans to reach beyond their immediate, practical needs is not just a luxury; it is an essential quality of being human.

3

People sense the value of music, even if they don't talk a lot about it. It is easy to assemble a large number of impressive statistics about the time and money people spend on music, the number of persons who attend concerts and buy recordings, the number who play musical instruments or sing in choirs, and so on. It is also easy to point out that music has been present in every society since the dawn of civilization. Furthermore, music is found in every part of the globe from the remote tribes of Africa and Australia to the city streets of Chicago and Beijing.

The importance of music to people is demonstrated in so many ways that it is easy to overlook them. Just about every film and television show has a sound track, which usually contains theme music. Music is included in public events such as the pregame activities at ball games, the celebrations of ship launchings, and the swearing-in ceremonies of public officials. People are exposed to music in supermarkets, in airports, and in their cars. The fact is that people can hardly get away from music.

A fundamental point is clear: *Music is important in people's lives.* The point may be obvious, but it is essential. If music were not important to people, then the teaching and learning of music would not be important. Music education would have no reason for being.

THE NEED FOR INSTRUCTION

The fact that music is important does not automatically ensure music's place in school curricula. It is quite possible to understand the value of music in people's lives but to fail to think that music should be taught in the schools. For example, a person might think that music can be learned casually in life, something like learning to ride a bicycle or to play cards. Such a view would be true *if* an education in music consisted only of learning to sing a few simple songs by rote. However, just as an education in mathematics consists of much more than learning how to add and subtract, and an education in science means more than observing the patterns in the weather, an education in music should involve much more than a little singing or superficial listening. Just as young people need to be taught reading, science, and history, they also need to be taught music.

The second major point is this: *The learning of any subject, including music, beyond rudimentary levels requires organized, systematic instruction, usually from a trained professional.* There is simply too much to be learned in today's world for areas of knowledge to be left to accidental circumstance of family or social conditions. The schools may not always do things as well as they should, but they fulfill a function in society that most families cannot. A system of education is necessary in today's complex societies. And for most students, if they are going to be educated in music, it will happen in the schools—or it won't happen at all.

Fortunately, most people not only value music, they also sense the value of young people learning music. Even if they can't express the reason why they think this is so, they feel it intuitively. When they hear a group of young people making music, even if it is not performed particularly well by musicians' standards, they know in their hearts that it is a good thing. Perhaps it is because of the feelings encouraged in them when they hear a group of young people doing something constructive, or perhaps they sense that music contributes to the quality of life in the community and its young people. Whatever their reasons are, most adults want young people to have a well-rounded education that includes music. Again, it is possible to assemble impressive statistics about the number of schools offering music programs, the amount of money raised by support groups for music activities, positive responses to opinion polls, and so on. The problem with support for music is not the availability of at least some music instruction in the schools, but rather the establishment of programs of sufficient scope and quality. Good school music programs cost more than most other areas of the curriculum, and competition is great for the limited funds available to education. In addition, music educators have not been diligent in educating school officials and the public about what a school music program should be like. This important matter is discussed in Chapter 10.

THE NATURE OF AESTHETIC EXPERIENCES

The word *music* covers a lot of territory. It runs from the tunes people whistle while painting a house, to pieces teenagers use to identify themselves with a particular group, to music created to inspire patriotic or religious feelings, to complex musical works that probe our psychological beings. It appears that there are many kinds of music for many different purposes, just as there are many different types of clothes, most of which are appropriate for only certain uses and occasions. Tuxedos and sweat suits are two examples of this fact.

Music, especially music for the concert or recital hall, can add a dimension to life that is available only through the arts. Whether one calls it "subjective reality," the "aesthetic world," the "world of feeling," "artistic" or "poetic," or something else, it has to do with thinking and experiences that are richer and often have more effect on people than rational, cognitive thinking. Sometimes these aesthetic experiences are more "true" in terms of expressing how people feel. Certainly they are a valuable aspect of human life. For example, the following lines from the Old Testament tell how the ancient Israelites will feel when they are freed from Babylon.

> *For you shall go out in joy,*
> *and be led forth in peace;*
> *the mountains and the hills before you*
> *shall break forth into singing,*
> *and all the trees of the field*
> *shall clap their hands.*

Taken literally, the lines don't make much sense. Everyone knows that trees have no hands and mountains can't sing. But in getting across the message of how the

Israelites will feel, the lines are far more expressive than merely saying, "You are going to feel mighty good when you are freed." Of course, everyday communication would be nearly impossible if only artistic, poetic discourse were used. But a life filled with only objective, rational thought would be pretty drab and tedious.

Aesthetic experiences differ from ordinary experiences in a number of ways. One basic difference between aesthetic and ordinary experiences is the nonpractical nature of aesthetic experiences. They are valued for the insight, satisfaction, and enjoyment they provide, not for any practical benefits. Looking at a bowl of fruit (a scene frequently painted by artists) is aesthetic when you contemplate the color and shape of the pieces of fruit; it is nonaesthetic when you are thinking about how the fruit reminds you that you are hungry. An aesthetic experience is an end in itself; it is done only for the value of doing it.

A second characteristic of an aesthetic experience is that both intellect and emotion are involved. When you look at a painting aesthetically, you are consciously aware of considering thoughtfully its shapes, lines, and colors. That is the intellectual part. At the same time you are reacting to what you see; you have feelings about the painting, even if it is abstract art. Seldom are these reactions so strong that you start laughing or crying, but you react to some degree; your feelings are involved.

Because intellectual contemplation is required, recreational activities, like playing tennis, or purely physical sensations, such as standing under a cold shower, are not considered aesthetic. Neither are purely intellectual efforts such as working multiplication problems, although even in that case a reaction is often involved, as when you see an error like $3 \times 9 = 28$.

A third characteristic of aesthetic experiences is the fact that they are experiences. You cannot tell someone about a painting or a musical work and expect that person to derive the same amount of enjoyment from the work as you did. In fact, telling about a piece of music or a drama seems to ruin it. For this reason aesthetic experiences have no answers, as do problems in a math class. Listening to the last minute of Beethoven's Fifth Symphony is not the "answer" to that symphony. Anyone who tries doing that is cheating himself or herself out of the aesthetic enjoyment that the symphony can provide.

A fourth characteristic of aesthetic experiences is a focusing of attention on the object being contemplated. This centering of attention is on the object as an object and not on a task to be accomplished, such as hitting the ball out of the infield in a baseball game.

Where does the idea of beauty enter into the discussion of aesthetic experiences? In one sense it doesn't enter in very much. Not all aesthetic experiences need be beautiful in the usual sense of the word. Hundreds of works of art, ranging from Stravinsky's *The Rite of Spring* to the Ashcan school of painting of Edward Hopper and George Bellows, have demonstrated that the aesthetic and the beautiful are two different considerations.

Pointing out what an aesthetic experience is *not* may help to clarify further what it *is*. The opposite of *aesthetic* is not ugly or unpleasant but rather might be thought of as "anesthetic"—no feeling, no life, nothing. Perhaps the clearest example of anesthetic behavior that comes to mind happened one day while I was observing a rather bad middle school band rehearsal. A sousaphone player was chatting with one of the drummers when the band director started up the band without waiting for the players who were not paying attention. After a few moments the young sousaphone player realized that he should be playing along with the others. Although he didn't know where they were in the music or what to play, he pulled the mouthpiece to his mouth and started blatting away without any sense of what was happening musically.

NONMUSICAL REASONS FOR MUSIC

Music has a long tradition of being included in schools for reasons such as citizenship, character development, team spirit, and health benefits. Plato, in his *Republic,* cites the need for music in the education of every citizen. His reasons were based on the ancient Greek idea of *ethos*—the belief that each mode promoted certain qualities of character in a person. Because music was closely allied with mathematics during the Middle Ages, music was one of the main subjects in medieval universities, and scholars were fascinated with the acoustical ratios of musical sounds. They wondered if the ratios might reveal secrets about the universe. In 1837, when Lowell Mason was given permission to begin music in the Boston schools, the subject was justified because it contributed to reading and speech and provided "a recreation, yet not a dissipation of the mind—a respite, yet not a relaxation—its office would thus be to restore the jaded energies, and send back the scholars with invigorated powers to other more laborious duties" (Birge, 1966, p. 43).

The belief that music has the power to help people in ways other than aesthetically did not end with Lowell Mason. In fact, until after the middle of the twentieth century nonmusical reasons were almost the only ones offered for music in the schools. For example, in 1941 Dykema and Gehrkens, two major figures in the development of American music education, wrote that "the teacher teaches the children through the medium of music" (pp. 380–381). The implication of their view is that music should be in the schools to help achieve goals beyond itself. In 1991 the report of the National Commission on Music Education devoted a number of pages to the notion that studying music contributes to success in school and in life.

Why is music so persistently justified on nonmusical grounds? Is it because those beliefs are true? Is it because music educators want solid practical reasons to establish a case for music in the schools? Or do they think that nonmusical reasons are more easily explained and understood than the "quality of life" argument? The answer may very well be, "all of the above." But the matter is not as simple as it may appear to be.

Music can contribute much to other areas of the curriculum, and this should happen more than it currently does in the schools. However, usually the matter of nonmusical values of music is more concerned with effects on individual students, and on something more than music's psychological value and the enrichment it can offer other school subjects.

Claims that something automatically transfers from music to other areas of curriculum or life are simplistic. To begin with, the nature of the instruction in music makes a lot of difference. Music sounds in and of themselves do not increase intelligence, help people to negotiate disagreements, or aid in preventing illnesses. Wolff carefully analyzed the available research on the transfer of learning in music to other subjects (Wolff, 1978). She found specific transfer only in language arts and some inadequate studies that indicate that there *may* be some other positive benefits of music study. Some benefits have also been observed in improved attitudes on the part of students toward school as indicated by a decline in absenteeism (Rodosky, 1974). Actually, some of this benefit may happen because music offers the students a refreshing change from what they are usually doing in school. Music probably is an effective "anti-monotony" activity.

There are many benefits from participation in music activities—performing before an audience, getting to know a teacher who is a good role model, achieving recognition in terms of an award, and so on. Such benefits are also available in other extracurricular activities. Some students find success in special clubs, others in athletics, others with the school paper, and others in music. One study of secondary school principals uncovered that over 70 percent of them could think of students who would have dropped out of school had it not been for the music and art programs (Florida Department of Education, 1990).

There is some additional intriguing evidence about music and success in school—and presumably then in life. Students who participate in music generally score higher on SAT examinations than students who are not in any arts courses. In 1989 the music students bettered the nonarts students 446 to 408 in the verbal measure and 491 to 467 in the quantitative measure (MENC, 1990).

On the surface those results would seem to prove once and for all that music has benefits beyond its artistic ones. Maybe. Music is good for people, but results such as higher SAT scores do not prove that music *causes* music students to be smarter. It could be that the smarter students gravitate toward music, which often does seem to be the case. Although it is difficult to prove in experimental research, it appears that some students get what might be called a "cycle of success" going in which already able and alert students enroll in music. In turn, this involvement helps them to become even more able, to become "winners." Whether this cycle of success is the result of attitude or ability or hard work doesn't matter. One accomplishment seems to fuel another, and for many high school students music is one area of accomplishment.

In making a case for music, music educators need to keep three facts in mind:

1. The research evidence supporting most claims of nonmusical value is very limited and some of it of questionable quality.

2. Many of the nonmusical benefits can be achieved better in areas other than music.

3. Nonmusical claims can divert attention away from the fact that music merits study regardless of any nonmusical benefits. Biology teachers, for example, do not claim that they teach something more than a knowledge of biology and science, and music does not need to make such claims either.

The avocational value of music becomes significant after students have completed high school. While the average life expectancy has been increasing, the average workweek has been decreasing. These facts mean that more time for leisure is available to people. Music is an important avocational activity in many countries, including America. One listing of community orchestras contains over 1600 entries, and there are thousands of church choirs and other amateur choral groups (American Symphony Orchestra League, 1991). An even greater number of people listen to music.

Two important points should be remembered about the nonmusical outcomes of music instruction:

1. *There are valid and supportable reasons for including music in the curricula of all schools, apart from any nonmusical benefits.* The nonmusical benefits should be thought of as "bonuses" for instruction that the schools should be offering anyway. The place of music in the schools does not depend on them, but its position may be stronger because of them.

2. *There is little a teacher can do directly to make these transfer, psychological, and avocational benefits happen.* The self-image of students, their social and psychological needs, and their choices of what to do with their leisure time are all influenced by circumstances over which teachers have little control. Teachers cannot use a teaching procedure that ensures any nonmusical benefits, although good teaching can help create a situation in which they are more likely to happen.

STUDENTS OR THE SUBJECT?

The fact that students can learn the subject of music while gaining personal and social benefits should lay to rest a long-standing but false dilemma: Should teachers teach the subject or the students? They should teach both; it is not an either-or proposition. Students are not helped if they are left ignorant about what they should know no matter what their personal situations may be. On the other hand, teachers cannot ignore the fact that they teach human beings. They need to be flexible and sensitive to the students' needs so that they can do the best possible job of teaching.

THE EXPERIENCE OF TEACHING

For music teachers, the rationales and the supporting data for music in the schools are reassuring, but logic and facts are not the primary reason for their choice of vocation. For them, teaching is a personal experience. It is a job that becomes meaningful and satisfying because of their experiences with young people. They remember students like the boy, who in spite of his small size, was determined to play trombone. Although it was tough going for him for a while, he learned to play it quite well, and he continued to do so throughout high school. They remember students like the nice boy who suffered somewhat from a palsied condition that left him with slurred speech and a tendency to become faint during performances of the high school choir. (Two husky boys were placed on each side of him to ease him down so that he could sit on the risers when he started feeling weak.) They remember how they were saddened a few years later upon hearing about his death from drowning while swimming, and they wondered, "Did I do all I could have done for him while he was in choir?" They remember others, too, including the fifth grade trumpet student who couldn't wait to try the valve oil the store had placed in his case. He was so eager to use it that he didn't wait for instructions and began administering the oil to the *outside* of the valves, and the oil soon ended up dribbling onto his lap. And they remember the hundreds of youngsters who were introduced to the music of Handel, Bartók, and Sousa and found in those works a world of music they hardly knew existed before. These and countless other experiences have convinced music teachers of the value of their work. They *know* music is well worth studying. No one need tell them that, although they enjoy hearing appreciative comments from parents, school administrators, or other teachers.

They also are aware of what their students would miss if there were no music instruction in the schools. They know that the students would be severely limited in what they know about music and their ability to be involved with it. A few students who possess unusual ability or come from families able and willing to pay for private instruction in music would be taken care of. However, most students would not have experience in an ensemble, be unable to understand music notation, have very limited skill in listening to music, know only a small number of songs of only one or two types, never have the chance to try creating some music, know little about an important aspect of Western civilization, and have much less favorable attitudes toward music. In short, they would be deprived—*cheated* may be a better word for it—of knowing about music beyond a very rudimentary level.

Because of their experiences in teaching and knowledge of what a good music program should be, most music teachers take their work seriously. As with any profession there are a few members who fall short, but the great majority of school music teachers are really able people who really care if their students learn. That is the way it should be, of course, but it can cause feelings of frustration and disappointment when a school administrator or parent appears to consider music in a lackadaisical way. The conscientious music teacher wonders: "Why don't they understand what the students are getting from their music classes?"

Music teaching is a personal matter for yet another reason. Often a music teacher is the only one in that area in the school, or at least the only one in the particular music specialty in the school. It's a rare high school that has two choral directors, for example. Professionally speaking, most music teachers feel somewhat alone. They seldom have a chance to discuss their work with another music teacher. This fact increases the importance of the Music Educators National Conference (MENC) and its state units for them. It also means that music teachers must be somewhat more self-directed and responsible than teachers of other subjects. Music teachers must generally be the developers, facilitators, and evaluators

---

MUSIC EDUCATORS' CREED

As a music teacher, I devote myself to two important causes:

1. Helping all people to make music a part of their lives, and
2. Advancing the art of music.

I believe that all people have the right to an education in music that:

*   teaches them the lifelong joy of making music through singing and playing instruments
*   gives them a chance to express through music what cannot be expressed in words
*   helps them to respond to music intellectually and emotionally
*   teaches them the language of music notation and opens the door to improvising, composing and arranging
*   equips them to make informed judgments about musical works and performances
*   educates them in the music of all cultures and historical eras
*   allows them to discover and develop their special talents, including preparing to make music their profession, if they so choose
*   prepares them to be involved with music throughout their lives

I teach music because—
> music makes a difference in the lives of people.

Figure 1.1   *Music Educators' Creed developed by Music Educators National Conference, 1991. (Source: Soundpost, 8 (3) (Spring 1992), p. 9)*

of their work. They must also be the communicators about their work to school administrators and parents to a degree not true of English or science teachers.

To voice the feelings about the value of teaching music, in 1991 the Music Educators National Conference developed a brief statement with which music teachers could remind themselves about the importance of their work. (See Figure 1.1.) It is a logical thought with which to conclude this chapter.

Questions

1. In what ways do people show that they value music?
2. Why can't young people just learn music on their own without being given music instruction in school?
3. What are the characteristics of aesthetic experiences?
4. Why don't music educators need to establish the fact that music has some nonmusical values in order to justify its place in the schools?
5. In what ways does music appear to have the greatest potential for nonmusical benefits?
6. What would most students miss if they did not receive music instruction in school?

Projects 1. Write a brief paragraph (100 words or less) saying why music needs to be taught in the schools.

2. Ask two persons who are currently teaching music in the schools to describe a few instances that helped convince them of the value of music classes and groups. Report your findings to the class.

References American Symphony Orchestra League. (1991). Washington, D.C.: Author.

Birge, E. B. (1966). *The history of public school music in the United States.* Reston, VA: Music Educators National Conference.

Data on music education (1990). Reston, VA: Music Educators National Conference.

Dykema, P. W., & Gehrkens, K. (1941). *The teaching and administration of high school music.* Evanston, IL: Summy-Birchard.

Growing up complete: the imperative for music education (1991). Reston, VA: Music Educators National Conference.

Rodosky, R. (1974). Arts IMPACT final evaluation report. Columbus, OH: Columbus Public Schools.

The role of fine and performing arts in high school dropout prevention (1990). Tallahassee, FL: Florida Department of Education.

Wolff, K. I. (1978). The nonmusical outcomes of music education: a review of the literature. *Council for Research in Music Education Bulletin 55.*

CHAPTER 2

The Nature of Music Teaching

W_{here} do you begin to become more able to analyze what music teachers do? A good place to start is a clear understanding about what the words *music* and *teach* really mean. Although their meanings may seem obvious, both have implications that are basic to what music teachers do, or at least what they should do.

WHAT IS MUSIC?

The nature of music seems like a simple matter, but is it? Is a crash of a cymbal or an eerie sound from an electronic instrument music? Why is a boom from a bass drum considered musical and booms from other sources thought of as noise? The difference is not so much in the sounds themselves as in the context in which they are heard. If they appear in a planned sequence of sounds, then they become music; if not, they are just random noises. The key to the matter is organization. In fact, music has often been defined as "organized sound."

The organizing of sounds in a span of time is something that human beings do. Music was not preordained by the cosmic laws of the universe and therefore something that people uncover. Music is created by humans for humans. It is a

human activity, and it varies in the forms it takes as much as other human creations like language, clothing, and food.

The world of music is vast and complex. Not only does it include all the music that people have created—folk, symphonic, instrumental, vocal, electronic, rock—it also encompasses musical activities such as singing, listening, analyzing, and creating. In fact, music is both a *product* in terms of being composed or improvised works and a *process* in terms of the actions involved in producing or reproducing music.

The vastness of the world of music forces teachers to make choices about what to teach and how to teach it. Fortunately, the definition of music as organized sound does offer a clue to the most important responsibility of music teachers: guiding students to understand and appreciate organized sounds. The processes of performing and creating music often help in achieving this goal. For example, creating melodies helps students to understand better the organizing of sounds, and so does singing or playing melodies on a clarinet.

Sometimes teachers emphasize one aspect of music so much that other aspects are largely ignored. Some teachers, for example, concentrate so much on the techniques of singing, playing, or creating music that the students never get around to understanding where the activity fits into the world of music. In other cases teachers devote so much attention to factual information that the students fail to think of music as an artistic experience.

Successful music teaching requires a balanced view of the world of music. Both musical objects *and* processes are needed, as is a variety in the type of music the students study. And both information and activities should be related to organized sound.

WHAT IS TEACHING?

Teaching is the organizing and guiding of the process in which students learn. Simply put, a teacher's role is to bring about the acquisition of information, understanding, and skills by the students. The way in which this role is accomplished can take a number of different forms. Sometimes it consists of providing the students with information, while at other times it involves setting up a learning situation and then stepping aside as the students work on their own. In some instances it means deciding on tasks for students to do individually, while in other cases it consists of leading a group in a unified effort such as singing a song. Whatever form the teaching takes, the essential characteristic is that the students learn. Results are what the process of teaching is all about, not the particular actions teachers take when working with students. The essential goal of teaching should not be confused with its different styles.

The definition of teaching as a process in which students learn also has implications for the attributes of teachers. Although a teacher may exhibit charm and good looks, lecture brilliantly, manage a classroom well, and use this or that method, if little learning takes place, he or she has not been successful as a teacher. In fact, occasionally (but not typically) a person who appears to violate the usual assumptions about what is needed to be a teacher turns out to be highly effective in getting students to learn. Teaching is so subtle and complex an endeavor that such a situation can happen every so often.

Teachers' jobs usually include duties in addition to leading the learning-teaching process—checking out instruments, taking attendance, keeping order in the classroom. Most of these duties are important and necessary, but they are not really part of the process. A person can be a good manager of classrooms and still not be a good teacher.

ANALYZING MUSIC TEACHING

Whether they realize it or not, almost all effective teachers have learned to think about teaching in an analytical way. They have an approach to the process of teaching. There is no one right way to examine teaching, but considering carefully its components is certainly a good one. When all is said and done, teaching comes down to five simple but basic components that can be stated as questions: (1) *Why* have music in the schools? (2) *What* should be taught in the music class? (3) *How* will it be taught? (4) *To whom* will it be taught? (5) *What are the results?* Each component is discussed in other chapters, but first a brief introduction to each.

A logical first step in thinking analytically about teaching is for you to observe music classes and analyze what the teacher does. This chapter contains a "practice analysis" form for a music class that you are currently taking. (See Figure 2.1.) Appendix A consists of a more extensive form for use when observing music teachers in the schools. Both forms focus your attention on what the teacher is doing. At this point you are not rendering general judgments about teachers. Before you do that, you need to look at what teachers do in a systematic way. The evaluation of music teachers as teachers should not be attempted until you are experienced in analyzing the process of teaching music.

Why Have Music in the Schools?

The most basic question concerns why there are music classes in the schools and teachers to teach them. That is why it was covered in Chapter 1. The answer to that question should provide teachers with a sense of direction, and to some degree it affects the answers to the other four questions of "What?," "How?," "To whom?," and "With what results?" Teachers who lack a clear understanding of what they are about are like rudderless ships floundering in the seas of education.

Fortunately, it is not necessary to return to the question of "Why?" when thinking about every class or rehearsal. If you can express your reasons for teaching music with a reasonable degree of confidence, your answer can give direction and consistency to your teaching. However, it is a good idea to rethink from time to time the fundamental reasons for teaching music. Maturity, experience, and changed circumstances call for a periodic review of a person's views. The topic is too important to be decided once and for all at the age of twenty. Develop some solid answers now to the question of why music should be taught in schools, but don't "chisel your beliefs in stone" this early in your career.

What Should Be Taught in Music?

The question of the content of music classes deals with the "stuff" of music— musical works, facts, fingerings, patterns of sound, understanding of the process of creating music, interpretation, and similar things. It includes all types of information, skills, and attitudes, and it should light the spark of creativity and individual expression within the students.

Deciding what to teach is an enormously complex matter. In addition, the world of music is huge, which makes choices about what to teach difficult. Other factors also contribute to the complexity of making these decisions, including practical considerations such as the musical background of the students, the amount of time available, the traditions of the community, the size of the class, and the amount and type of materials available.

Music teachers should also remember that students learn not only in music classes or under the guidance of teachers. After all, students spend only about 1000 of their 8736 hours each year in school, so it is not reasonable to credit or blame

ON-CAMPUS OBSERVATION FORM

All of you have the good fortune to be taking a music theory and/or a music history course. Since you are attending this class anyway, it is a convenient one for gaining skill in analyzing the teaching process (*not* the instructor!). Select one class from either of these areas for this assignment. Then, analyze the teaching process by answering the following five questions:

1. Why? What is the reason for this course and the material it covers?

2. What? What specifically are the students in the class supposed to be learning?

3. How? What method or methods is the instructor using to teach the content to the students?

4. To whom? What appear to be the musical backgrounds and interests of the students in the class?

5. Results? What actions, if any, did the instructor take to determine how well the students had learned what was being taught? If such actions were taken, how well did it appear that the students had learned?

Figure 2.1   *On-Campus Observation Form for practice analysis.*

the school for everything students learn or know. The fact remains, however, that not much learning or understanding of music will usually take place without organized, competent instruction in school.

Unlike the question of "Why?" the matter of what to teach needs to be spelled out specifically for each lesson or class. It isn't enough merely to "put in time" in music. There should always be clearly stated objectives in terms of what the students are to learn.

How Should Music Be Taught?

The question of how music is taught focuses on the ways of organizing and structuring instruction, as well as selecting the manner of presentation. Some people who have never taught falsely assume that teaching is a job in which you merely stand up in front of the students and talk. If that were the case, teaching would indeed be easy! However, that is not the way it is, even if some experienced teachers make it look easy, like a fine violinist who makes the difficult passages of a concerto sound effortless.

The suggestions in methods textbooks are geared to what might be called the "typical" school situation. Readers should realize, however, that there are almost no typical schools, and certainly each student is unique. The ideas presented apply to perhaps a majority of teaching situations. As much as an author would like to, it is impossible to offer specific ideas on how to teach music in each of the thousands of schools in the United States.

The difficulty in specifying procedures for all situations is not characteristic of several other professions. For example, because nearly everyone's appendix is in approximately the same part of the body, surgeons are taught a specific surgical procedure for its removal. Unfortunately, human behavior is much less consistent than human anatomy. Not all students have the same interests, musical background, and mental ability. For this reason identical teaching procedures sometimes produce the opposite results in different classrooms, especially when different teachers are involved. Part of the challenge of teaching is being adaptable enough to meet a variety of situations.

Deciding on which methods are most appropriate for teaching specific material to a particular group of students is one of the challenges of teaching. Suppose a teacher wishes to teach a second grade class to sing a song with pleasing tone and accurate pitch. Because the song is simple, it presents the teacher with no technical obstacles. The children are enjoyable to work with and tractable, offering the teacher few problems in guiding the class. The challenge comes in presenting the art of music so that it becomes meaningful to the seven-year-old youngsters. How can the contour of the melodic line be impressed on children who don't know what the word *contour* means? How does a teacher make second graders conscious of the pitches and accurate when they sing them? Certainly not by merely telling them, "Watch your intonation!" How can the phrases of the song be presented so that the students will understand better the function of phrases in the song? Does a gentle sweep of the arm really aid children in perceiving phrases, or are there other means that would be more effective? These questions have just scratched the surface of the pedagogical questions involved in teaching a song.

A sizable amount of information exists about learning and the conditions under which it takes place, but much remains to be uncovered. This available information should be the "stuff" of music methods courses. Ideas on teaching change as new evidence becomes available from research and practical experience. For example, it was once believed that language reading should be introduced by teaching letters of the alphabet first, since words are made up of letters. When the alphabet had been learned, they were put into words and finally into sentences (Swaby, 1984). This method (known as the ABC method) seems logical, but what is logical is not always the way people function. Today teachers know that words are comprehended as a whole, not letter by letter. Without this knowledge and without training in how to use it, teachers would waste much time and introduce habits that would have to be broken later. A fluent reading ability and a gracious way with children are not sufficient qualifications for teaching reading. The same is true of teaching music.

To Whom Is Music Being Taught?

Music is taught to someone, and the capabilities and motivation of the students are essential components in the teaching process. Not only must teachers consider such obvious matters as the range of voices and previous musical knowledge, but they should also be aware of the probable use the students will make of what they learn. A seventh grade general music class and a high school orchestra may both study a Bach fugue, but each will approach the work in a different way and with a different degree of technical information.

The "To whom?" question requires that teachers put themselves in the place of the students in order to recognize better their varied interests, needs, and backgrounds. Teachers must try to see the subject through the eyes of the pupils. This ability is needed not only to know how to adapt methods and materials but also to establish a teacher-class relationship that will encourage a positive attitude in the students. Students are often slow to distinguish between their feelings toward the teacher and their feelings toward the subject. And in a subject such as music, in which so much depends on feeling and perception, the students' attitudes are especially important. When the students realize that the teacher is sensitive to their interests, the relationship between pupils and teacher is greatly improved, and more learning takes place.

What Are the Results?

The fifth component in the teaching process is finding out the results of a class or lesson. What do the students know or what are they able to do after the class that they did not know or do before? Exactly and precisely, what was accomplished?

Teachers cannot determine the amount of learning by trusting to luck or by watching the students' facial expressions. Instead what is needed is evidence in terms of what students can do as a result of the learning experience. The term *observable behavior* does not refer to classroom deportment, although there is some relationship between the quality of teaching and classroom conduct. Instead, it refers to specific learning revealed through the students' abilities to answer questions, to signal when a theme returns, to sing or play the third of a triad when asked, or to add an improvised phrase to a line of music.

Why? What? How? To whom? With what results? The answers to these questions are the essential parts of the process called teaching. If teachers fail to think through each one of these questions, they run the risk of producing educational failures marked by wasted time and lost opportunities for the students. Teaching is similar in this respect to getting an airplane off the ground. If any important part is missing or not working, the plane will not take off. Because educational failures are less dramatic and less immediately visible than airplanes failing to become airborne, some teachers are able to hold their jobs without thinking carefully about what they are doing. But their students are the losers! Sometimes the material is too difficult, too easy, or meaningless; sometimes the hours spent in music classes add up to little additional knowledge or skills for the students; sometimes teachers and classes wander, not knowing what they are trying to accomplish or if the students have learned anything. When any of these situations occurs, the lack of learning can correctly be called an "educational failure."

The five components provide an approach for thinking and learning about teaching. They also give focus to thoughts that could otherwise be a formless blob in one's mind. Analyzing and understanding the teaching process are the first steps in becoming a good teacher.

PLANNING FOR MUSIC TEACHING

Good teaching not only requires thinking through the five questions in the teaching process, it also calls for developing into plans the answers to those questions. Teachers need to be organized about what they intend to teach.

The reasons for planning in teaching any subject may be so obvious that they are sometimes overlooked. The main reason planning is done is to enable teachers to know what they are trying to accomplish and how they will accomplish it. Without planning, teachers are not clear about what they want to teach or the methods they will use to help the students learn.

There are other benefits of planning. One benefit is the feelings of confidence and security it encourages, which usually helps a teacher be more effective. Another benefit of planning is that time and effort are not wasted because of uncertainty and confusion. Time is usually wasted when teachers try improvising in front of a class.

Amount of Planning by Music Teachers

Many music teachers, especially those who direct performing groups, do not do much planning; in fact, a few teachers seem to do none at all, except for the setting of some dates for performances and other nonteaching matters. Planning is not a popular topic in the music education profession. If planning has the benefits just described, then why do music teachers not do more of it? There are several likely reasons. One is that some music teachers see the function of school music as the providing of entertainment instead of the education of students. As long as the students seem to be having a good time, these teachers are not worried about learning.

Some teachers wonder if anyone cares whether the students in their classes learn much about music. Sometimes, or so it seems, the principal is favorably impressed if there are few complaints about music class from the students and almost never is anyone sent to the office for disciplinary reasons. Other music teachers and some parents want a performing group to win high ratings at contests or present entertaining performances, and they don't care about other aspects of music education. In other words, the rewards (or reinforcement, to use a psychological term) to teachers for teaching students about music are not strong in many situations.

Many music teachers carry a heavy teaching load. They hurry from one class to another for six hours a day, and after school they have special rehearsals or they help students. There simply is not much time or energy left for planning by the end of the day.

There are aspects of music teaching that cannot be fully planned for. When teaching a song in two parts to a general music class, no one can predict exactly how well the class will sing the song or the places where mistakes will occur. Therefore, the teacher must make some on-the-spot decisions, regardless of the amount of prior planning.

Some music teachers are suspicious of planning because they think it might encourage teaching that lacks flexibility and spontaneity. This might be true if teachers were unwilling to make any changes in their plans or allowed their plans to shackle their enthusiasm and adaptability. Clearly, if it seems wise to alter a plan and it appears that the students will learn more if a change is made, then no teacher should hesitate to change what has been planned. Although some plans may be altered before they are used, the original planning was not a waste of time. The unused planning was a foundation on which the teacher built a better lesson; it provided something for the teacher to work from, which is better than stumbling about without objectives and ideas of how to achieve them.

Aids in Planning

It is not a sign of weakness or incompetence to take advantage of books and curriculum guides in planning, especially if you are not an experienced teacher. Music teachers in the secondary schools see five or sometimes six classes a day, and elementary music specialists often teach music at six different grade levels and see each classroom twice a week. That amount of teaching requires a lot of planning. A new teacher has no reservoir of ideas from previous years, so an even greater effort in planning is required. Any help that a teacher can utilize in planning and teaching should not be avoided.

Several sources are available that provide suggestions and ideas on which teachers can build. Some school districts have developed curriculum guides or courses of study for parts of their music curriculum. Some of these guides are useful, but others are very general and of limited value to teachers. Many states publish curriculum guides, some of which can be a source of ideas for teachers. Elementary and middle school music specialists can take advantage of the ideas offered in the music series books. These books contain not only materials and lessons but also suggestions and teaching aids. Teachers need not use everything in a book or guide; they can choose what will be useful to them and omit portions that are not of value.

Long-Range Planning

Where does a teacher start in planning for an entire school year? Because this is no easy task, the beginning teacher should feel free to take ideas from any source—books, curriculum guides, and other teachers. But what kind of ideas? Ideas about what you want the students to learn, to be able to do.

At the beginning these ideas may be general and vague. They need to be honed and sharpened so that they can be stated clearly and in terms of student actions. For example, suppose you have an idea that you would like to see the students understand and read music notation better. That is a perfectly good but vague notion. The next step is to state the idea in specific terms so that you can express more clearly what you want them to know about or do with notation. It might be that among other things you want them to become conscious of the size of intervals in a melody. You hope they notice that adjacent intervals sound closer than wide intervals, and you also hope that the students can identify the basic intervals such as thirds and fifths when they see and hear them. What began as a general guide has now become more specific.

Although it may not be easy to "fill in the blanks" for classes meeting a couple of months in the future, teachers should attempt to plan for an entire semester or school year. Long-term planning allows for thinking through the sequence in which topics will be presented. Without such plans, gaps or duplication probably will occur. For example, one teacher was teaching about the jazz influences in music and wanted to have the students learn about blue notes. When he got to the point where he wanted to explain how the third, fifth, and seventh notes of the scale are lowered, he realized that the students did not know the pattern of the major scale.

Planning for a course or a school year concentrates on the main topics and their order of appearance. Making detailed lesson plans for classes that will be taught three months in the future probably is a waste of time, because changes will be needed by the time the plans are to be taught. For these reasons, prospective and beginning teachers should think of long-term planning as the first step. They should expect to make changes in them; in fact, they can expect to make quite a few changes.

Unit Planning

In a sense, planning for a group of classes or rehearsals is halfway between planning for a course and planning for just one class. Unit plans have elements of long-term planning in that they cover three or more classes, but they are much more specific about what will be taught and how it will be taught. Sometimes the plans for a small number of classes or rehearsals can be written at the same time.

The idea of unit planning makes it possible for a topic to act as a unifying thread for a number of classes. A topic is not treated in just one short presentation but rather is developed and studied in enough depth to help the students remember it better.

One guideline that music teachers should follow in developing or selecting units is that they be centered on something to do with music. Rather than selecting a group of songs about rivers or lines from plays, both of which are nonmusical topics, units in general music classes should be about sound, types of music, uses of music, playing or singing, and so on. The difference between building around a musical or a nonmusical topic may seem like hairsplitting, but it can lead to quite different types of lessons. In the case of the nonmusical topic, music is included when appropriate for the topic. In the case of a musically centered unit, other information is included as it pertains to the music being studied.

Because class situations vary greatly, and because each unit for a general music class has its own particular requirements, it is impossible to provide a model plan that can be used for all units. Essentially the unit should focus on some phase of music and integrate as much as possible the activities of singing, listening, creating, discussing, and reading. It is neither possible nor desirable for every unit to encompass in each class period the wide variety of activities that could be included. Some topics suggest singing, while others invite discussion and study. Teachers should not strain to achieve subject matter integration where it does not logically exist. If a unit does not in itself suggest appropriate songs, then the class can work on songs that are not directly related to the unit and that will not detract from the unit. When possible, videotapes, books, bulletin board displays, field trips, and appearances by outside authorities should be integrated into the unit of study—not forcibly, but as a logical extension of the learning experience.

The rehearsals of performing groups can also be planned in units. If, as is hoped, the course of study consists of more than preparing for one public performance after another, then units can be formed around types of music, forms, or technical problems. For example, a unit for studying choral music could be formed about particular aspects of works from Russia or the Renaissance, a unit of band music developed around overtures, and a unit for orchestras created around types of bowing. While such learning is going on, the group is also rehearsing some of the music for performance.

Lesson Planning

When all is said and done, lesson planning is merely the process of organizing the things a class will do to learn music. Although several approaches can be used to develop lesson plans for teaching music, certain guidelines should be considered:

1. Consider what most of the students know and what would be worthwhile for them to learn in music. Finding out the students' present knowledge or skills may involve giving a test. However, because of practical limitations of time and energy, music teachers cannot do this very often. Furthermore, after a teacher has taught a group of students for a while, he or she should have a rather clear idea about what the students know and can do musically. In performing groups each performance of music provides the teacher with information about what the group can do. Observing student responses to questions and other learning activities provides some information in music classes. Although teachers need not give formal pretests often, they should consciously look for and consider where the students are in terms of the subject and what has been covered in previous classes.

2. Select two or three specific topics or skills to teach in music classes, or one specific topic or skill in each rehearsal. Students, especially those in elementary and middle school, become restless and their attention wanes if any one activity is continued for too long a period of time. One activity is satisfactory for rehearsals because a lot of time is spent playing or singing.

3. State the points to be studied specifically. An objective such as "to learn about music composed in the Renaissance style" is too vague and too broad. An objective such as "to identify aurally and in notation the points of imitation in Renaissance madrigals and motets" is much clearer and more manageable.

4. Formulate the objectives for the class or group in terms of what the students should be able to do as a result of the instruction. Unless the students can provide evidence of how much they have learned, it is hard for a teacher to determine what should be taught in subsequent classes. Objectives can apply to skills as well as to information. For example, "The group will learn to sing Palestrina's 'Sanctus' with a light tone and accurate pitch." Other objectives can apply to learning with a criterion level added if the teacher so desires; for example, "Ninety percent of the students will be able to locate in the notation three examples of imitative entrances in 'Sanctus' by Palestrina."

5. Select appropriate materials. The teacher who wishes to teach about Renaissance madrigals should try to secure the most authentic version of each madrigal that is available and to play recordings of madrigals being sung in an authentic style.

6. Decide on how the content is to be taught. Suppose that a class is learning to identify *A B A* form. There are several ways in which this could be done. If the class knows a song that is in *A B A* form, they could sing it through and identify the different sections. A recording of a work with clearly delineated sections in *A B A* could be played. The students could create a simple piece in three-part form using classroom instruments. They might think of ways to represent visually the different sections of a piece of music, such as with different symbols or colors for the various sections of the work. Each of these ways—and many others—is appropriate under the right circumstances.

7. Assess the results of each portion of a class or rehearsal. Teachers should gather some evidence on how well the students have learned what was taught.

The exact manner in which a lesson plan is put down on paper is not of major importance, but planning for the main points to be taught is. What follows is a sample plan built around the basic questions of what, how, and with what results. In the sample plan these questions are indicated along the left-hand side of the page by the words "Objectives," "Materials," "Procedures," and "Assessment of Results." Notice that the categories are used for both of the main topics to be presented in the lesson. Estimates of the amount of time to be consumed by a topic are also included. Such estimates provide a teacher with some guidance on how much time to spend but should not be followed slavishly. The "If time permits" heading allows for some latitude in using time and saves a teacher from the uncomfortable position of completing the planned lesson with ten or more minutes of class time remaining.

Sample Lesson Plan for General Music

Objectives

1. Learn about the music and words of typical ballads.
2. Become informed about the gestures used in conducting, the conductor's score, and interpretations and how they differ.

Materials

1. *Music and You, 7,* and recordings.

Procedures

1. Ballad (15 minutes):
   a. Review "Henry Martin" (*Music and You,* p. 41) by singing the song again. Give the class the seventh and eighth verses.
   b. Ask if most songs they sing express feelings or tell a story. Discuss the text. Does it tell a story? Is it happy? Does it repeat lines or words? Does it contain any words they don't understand?
   c. Ask about the characteristics of music. Does it need much accompaniment? Does it have several verses to the same melody? Does it contain any portions that are similar or the same? Is it highly expressive music? What's unusual about the rhythm?
   d. Listen to the recording of "Henry Martin."

e. Sing the song again with improved expression and style.

2. Conductor (25 minutes):
   a. Read and discuss the pages on conducting in *World of Music* (pp. 89–94).
   b. Discuss the musical directions of conductors. Point out how the size and style of gestures give an idea of the style of the music.
   c. Study the page of the score of "O Fortuna" from Orff's *Carmina Burana,* and explain any words the students don't know.
   d. Play the recording of the two versions of "O Fortuna." Which is faster? Louder? How does the tone quality differ between them?
   e. Ask if one version is better than the other or just different. Discuss personal preferences and their validity.

3. If time permits (5 minutes): Review "Frog Went A-Courtin' " (*Music and You,* p. 122). Compare with "Henry Martin." Discover what chords are used in the accompaniment.

Assessment of Results

As a result of the lesson, the students will be able to:

1. Describe the characteristics of storytelling, strophic form, rather detached quality in the ballad, and find similar measures. (Check for participation in singing.)
2. Describe how conducting gestures reflect style of music, describe the basic pattern of an orchestral score, and state differences between two versions of "O Fortuna."

Lesson plans can be arranged in several different formats. One has just been presented. Another example, shown in Figure 2.2, presents a different type of format in which the information is to be written in columns according to the portion of the teaching process.

Lesson plans should not be like scripts for a play that teachers read almost line by line to a class. Such plans are very time-consuming to prepare, and few people can read a lecture to a class and make it seem interesting and vital. Some materials available to teachers do provide ready-made questions and lines to read

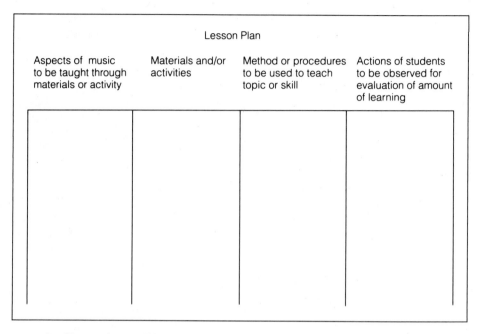

Figure 2.2   *Example of lesson plan in which the information is to be written in columns.*

to the class; these are the actual content of a lesson, not plans for a lesson. There is a difference between a plan and something to read.

Planning for Rehearsals

To prepare for rehearsals, teachers must decide (1) which pieces will be studied, (2) which places in the music should receive special attention, and (3) what should be accomplished or learned in conjunction with the music. In addition, teachers need to study the score and parts to the music they don't already know. The teacher studies the music prior to class or rehearsal to analyze it, to learn the score, to work on any special conducting techniques, and to decide on the best interpretation of the work. Also, the study should anticipate spots that are likely to be difficult for the group. When the students reach a troublesome passage, teachers should be quick to come up with the alternative fingering for G on the trumpet, a bowing technique that will help the strings to coordinate the bow with the left hand, or a suggestion for getting the woodwinds to play a particular rhythmic figure correctly. *No teacher or conductor should be caught unprepared for such problems; plans should have been made for overcoming them.*

No outline of activity is suitable for all rehearsals of performing groups. The methods and content should vary according to what the students have learned previously, the closeness of a performance, and the type of music being studied. Many teachers begin rehearsals with a combination warm-up and technique-developing routine. This portion of the rehearsal should be varied from day to day and be relevant to the other activities in the course. In singing, for example, attention can be centered on producing the sound correctly or singing in tune. In instrumental music, playing techniques can be stressed, or a scale or exercise can be played to practice correct fingerings or bowings. Warm-up activity should be brief—not longer than five to seven minutes.

To close a class, the students can review something they do well or put together something on which they have been working. The idea is not to leave the group hanging in the middle of learning a piece of music when the period ends. Between the opening and closing of the rehearsal, the group can begin studying new music, review familiar works, perfect its current repertoire, and learn aspects of music theory and literature relevant to the music being rehearsed.

It is probably possible to get by without spending time in planning for teaching. However, music educators should set their goals higher than just getting by. If students in music classes and performing groups are to learn the most they can in the time available, teachers need to plan carefully for what they will do. And good planning and teaching are based on an understanding of the process involved with teaching.

ASSESSING LEARNING IN MUSIC

The assessment of what students have learned in a music class or rehearsal is the other side of the coin from planning. The two aspects of teaching are, or should be, that closely related. In fact, assessment is not even possible unless the objectives have been clearly stated. As the saying goes, "If you don't know where you're going, you can't tell if you get there."

Reasons for Assessing

Why is it important for teachers to assess what their students have learned? First, it's simply one component of good teaching. Teachers need to have some information about how well the students have achieved the objectives. Without such knowledge, teachers are forced to rely on impressions, hunches, and assumptions. Sometimes these subjective ways are accurate, but more often they are not. Teaching without assessing is like driving around a strange city with no map; you may make it to your destination, but some luck will be needed to do so. With the knowledge assessment provides, teachers can decide much more intelligently what to do next. It may be that more work is needed on some point, or that another approach is needed, or that the material is too difficult, or any one of many possible reasons. At least a teacher will not continue to be ineffective due to a lack of information about how effectively something was learned.

A second reason for assessing learning is the evidence of learning that it can provide. Educational agencies and school boards are becoming increasingly interested in knowing what the students have learned in various courses. They want to know the results, the "bottom line." Their attention to the visible results of learning may be shortsighted, but it is understandable.

A third reason for assessing learning is that it can lead to more valid grading of students. Assessing and grading are not the same thing, but by providing information, assessment contributes to better grading.

Ways of Assessing

Doing assessment well is not easy, because it is not possible to measure many aspects of learning directly. For example, the concept of *musicianship* is not something that can be weighed, seen, or held in the hand. It exists only as a concept or mental construct in people's minds. To most people, actions such as performing the music accurately, phrasing at suitable places, and changing dynamic levels carefully and sensibly are indications of it. However, no two people mean exactly the same thing when they use the word *musicianship*. This situation presents a problem, because people look for slightly different things in musicianship. What, then, can be measured about musicianship or any mental construct? The answer is *indicators*. Indicators of musicianship probably include keeping a steady tempo, performing in tune, phrasing at the right places, using an appropriate tone quality, and so on. It is very unlikely that a student who plays with poor intonation, breaks up phrases, and seldom varies the dynamic level will be considered musical. Although seeking evidence about indicators of something does not solve all the assessment problems (for example, some people may not agree that keeping a steady beat or knowing where a breath should be taken are valid indicators), such evidence is far more valid in assessing learning than is trying to deal with general ideas.

Assessing the effectiveness of instruction does not mean giving one test after another. It is not necessary to involve all the members of the class in every evaluation situation. A sample of four or five students selected at random to answer questions or in other ways indicate what they are learning is usually enough to provide a good idea of how much learning is taking place.

Questions

1. What makes some groups of sounds music and other groups of sounds noise?

2. In what ways is music both a *product* (an object that exists in sound) and a *process* (actions that create or make music)?

3. What are the questions that imply the basic elements of the teaching process?

4. Why is it difficult to spell out in any detail the procedures for teaching music?

5. What is an observable behavior? Why are observable behaviors valuable for teachers in analyzing the teaching process?

6. Why do music teachers, including directors of performing groups, need to plan for their classes and rehearsals?

7. What are the seven points to cover in making plans for classes and rehearsals?

Project   Think of something that a music teacher typically teaches a class or performing group. Next, think of a class or group to which to teach that aspect of music. Then, answer the following questions:

1. Why is it useful for the students to learn that fact or skill?

2. Precisely what about that aspect of music are the students to learn?

3. How could that fact or skill best be taught to the group of students you have in mind?

4. How can a teacher tell how well the students have learned what they were supposed to learn?

Reference   Swaby, B. E. R. (1984). *Teaching and learning reading.* Boston: Little, Brown.

CHAPTER 3

The Qualities and Competencies of Music Teachers

A_{re} people born with the ability to teach music well, or do they become good teachers by hard work and self-improvement? What characteristics do most good music teachers possess? Where do preprofessional experiences and student teaching fit into the training of teachers? These and other questions are concerned with the type of persons music teachers should be, the skills and knowledge they need to have, and the ways they can continue to improve their ability to teach after they get a job. Because music programs can be no stronger than the people who teach them, the quality of music teachers is vitally important.

One purpose of an introductory course in music education is to encourage you to think about what makes a good music teacher. Some of what is involved with such thinking concerns what a music teacher *does,* and part of it concerns what a music teacher *is* in terms of personal qualities and attributes.

PERSONALITY AND EGO

The research and writings on the topic of the personality of good teachers have tended to reaffirm what nearly everyone already knows: Warm, friendly, understanding teachers are more effective than those who aren't; businesslike and orga-

nized teachers are more effective than teachers who are careless and disorganized; and imaginative and enthusiastic teachers surpass in effectiveness those who are routine and dull.

A few points can be stated with confidence, however, about the personality of successful music teachers. They should be adults in the fullest sense of the word, and they should be conscious of the needs and feelings of others. The whims and idiosyncrasies of an "artistic" temperament have no place in the schools.

It does seem that music teachers are susceptible to greater ego-involvement in their work than are most other teachers. It may be that the "leader" role that many music teachers have as part of their jobs attracts people with greater ego needs. It could be that the circumstances of the job tend to encourage a heightened sense of personal involvement. It may be that some music teachers would rather be performers. Whatever the reasons, many music teachers tend to view their work as an extension of themselves. For example, a number of times the author has heard music teachers almost boastfully relate how the choir or band "fell apart" after they left a particular teaching position. Some teachers work hard with students who have ability because they help bring recognition to the teacher, but they have little time for the less talented students. The situation pictured in the comic strip on page 34 in which the teacher draws attention to himself or herself has

actually happened in football programs and yearbooks; only the size of the director's face was less prominent.

Music teachers need to face the fact that the pressures of ego involvement will be present throughout their teaching career. What they need to do—and do often—is remind themselves that the role of teacher is one in which you gain satisfaction through observing the learning of your pupils. Music exists in the schools for the benefit of the students, not for the aggrandizement of teachers. The *Final Report* of the Teacher Education Commission of the Music Educators National Conference (MENC) makes the point clearly. "The ego-satisfaction of the music student in college is often gained through personal performance whereas that of the music educator is gained largely from creating opportunities for students' music expression" (Klotman, 1972, p. 5).

The preceding paragraph about where the satisfactions in teaching are found may sound like a teacher's role is one of self-sacrifice. That would not be the correct conclusion. It is not so much a sacrifice of ego and self as it is a different way of achieving satisfaction. When you teach so that the students learn something they would not have learned without your efforts, that is truly gratifying. There is something deeply satisfying about knowing that you make a difference in the lives of people, especially young people. Such satisfactions can hardly be thought of as making a sacrifice; far from it. They are much more rewarding than a career devoted to beating out someone for better chairs in an orchestra or roles in operas. When all is said and done, there is a lot more enjoyment in doing something for others than in worrying so much about oneself, and such activity carries with it its own type of ego-satisfaction.

The grooming and appearance of teachers is a subject that has occasionally produced heated discussions, but it probably has little effect on the students' learning *as long as it does not distract from or interfere with the respect and confidence the students have in the teacher.* It is everyone's right as a citizen to wear any hairdo or clothing style they wish. But if a person's appearance causes the students to look upon the teacher as a freak or egoist, then it is simply not worth the loss of learning that results. Each college and each school has its own standards, both written and unwritten, on this matter. New teachers and student teachers should find out what those expectations are and abide by them. In most cases, common sense is a reliable guide for personal appearance.

The speaking voice of teachers should be pleasing, and, more important, it should carry a quality of decisiveness. During student teaching the complaint is sometimes leveled at a novice teacher that his or her voice cannot be heard in the back of the room. This problem usually disappears as the beginning teacher gains confidence and experience and makes an effort to improve in this area.

In the final analysis there is a quality beyond personality, grooming, and voice: a sense of commitment to being a good teacher. David Ausubel, the noted educational psychologist, has written: "Perhaps the most important personality characteristic of a teacher . . . [is] . . . the extent of the teacher's personal commitment to the intellectual development of students. . . . It determines in large measure whether he will expend the necessary effort to teach for real gains in the intellectual growth of pupils or will merely go through the formal motions of teaching" (1978, p. 506). Myron Brenton is more blunt about it: "The best teachers wear a large invisible button that reads, 'I give a damn'" (1970, p. 40).

The Importance of Being Yourself

When authors or groups write about what teachers should be like, they are presenting an ideal or model, not a set of minimum competencies that must be met. They realize that teachers are human beings and that no one can fulfill every suggested quality. The reason that all the qualities are mentioned is to make readers aware of what is desirable in a music teacher.

Every one of us has strong and weak points in terms of being a teacher. It is obvious that we should utilize our strengths to the fullest in order to compensate for our weaker points. With some teachers their strength is their ability to play piano, with others it is an ability to inspire students, and with others it is their knowledge of music and their intelligence. Each person develops different ways to fulfill the role of teacher. Figure 3.1 contains a form that will help you in looking at your strong and your weak points in terms of being a music teacher.

Many young teachers who have studied under a dynamic, extroverted individual or observed such a person in full swing at a workshop may have wondered, "Is it necessary for me to have that kind of personality to be successful?" Extroversion does not guarantee a teacher's ability to convey ideas and teach effectively. Suppose a teacher puts on a red shirt and conducts groups something like a cheerleader. At first that would probably grab the attention of the students, but what about the fiftieth or hundredth class? What was once attention grabbing could become pretty annoying. And what does the red-shirted teacher do *then* to get attention?

Many good music teachers are not extroverts and would only look silly if they tried to be. Instead of extroversion what is needed is a quality of decisiveness, of

SELF-EVALUATION AS A MUSIC TEACHER

1. What *personal* characteristics do you possess that you think will help you become a successful music teacher?

2. What *personal* characteristics do you possess that should be strengthened so that you can become a successful music teacher?

3. What *musical* attributes do you possess that will help or hinder you in being a successful music teacher?

4. What aspects of teaching music are most attractive to you?

5. What aspects of teaching music are least attractive to you?

6. Do you think that you get along well with people—all kinds of people—even those who are quite different from yourself?

Figure 3.1   *Self-evaluation form*

7. Do you like children and young people, even when they don't behave the way you would like them to?

8. Are you a fairly well organized person?

9. Do you enjoy it when other people succeed, or does it bother you when they do?

10. If you could make the same amount of money singing or playing as a performer as you could teaching music, would you rather perform or teach? Can you explain the choice you made in answer to that question?

11. Do you tend to be interested mostly in music, or are you also quite interested in other arts and in other areas of study such as languages and literature, social sciences, and physical sciences?

knowing what is needed, and letting the students know that you are competent and in charge. Good teachers cannot be weak and timid. The way in which each individual achieves this quality of competence depends on his or her unique personality, but it must be achieved, especially when teaching in the secondary schools. Two conditions can help achieve the impression of competence: (1) a firm belief that what you are teaching is worth the students' knowing and (2) the confidence that arises from understanding what you are about as a teacher. Beyond these basic understandings the quality of decisiveness (not aggressiveness—there is a difference) is something that many future teachers must work on and develop through experience and training.

Human Qualities and Professional Competence

It is easy to point out that teachers should be sensible, fair, decisive, and interested in the students' learning. But how do these attributes relate to the ability of teachers to work with people, something that is central to teaching? Here are some thoughts on the question.

- Music educators, like all teachers, need to be ever growing in their outlook on their work and on their students. They continue to learn until they retire from teaching. They look for and consider new ideas carefully, and they are not afraid to try different approaches to old problems.

- They relate well to other human beings, especially their students. They empathize with their students and colleagues. They can relate to people of differing cultural backgrounds.

- They can relate the subject matter of music to other academic disciplines, especially the other arts. They see music as a part of the larger culture.

- They understand their role as teacher. They gain satisfaction, not from receiving personal attention but rather from seeing growth and success in their students. They realize that they need to lead and inspire their students, but they also realize they should not dominate the class or rehearsal room.

- They are musician-teachers. They realize that they fail their students if they don't teach them musical skills and understandings, as well as favorable attitudes toward music. They seek out a variety of music for study and performance, and they value the music for its expressive qualities.

Personal Efficiency. Proper planning requires personal efficiency and organization. Unless teachers have these qualities, both they and their students are apt to find themselves in a state of confusion. Music teachers have been known to forget to order chairs or risers for a performance, to lose their own music, to fail to keep track of uniform and instrument numbers (or worse yet, money from ticket sales!), and to wait to the last moment to prepare a program for a concert. What excitement these fumblings create! But when confusion reigns, the educational results are reduced. Musicians, along with almost everyone else, may dislike "administrivia"; but trivial or not, details must not be neglected.

Relations with Professional Colleagues. In some instances, a music program is hampered because of poor relationships between music teachers and the people with whom they work. For example, if a teacher is personally disagreeable, the school guidance counselors may be hesitant about encouraging students to enroll in music courses. Some instrumental music teachers consider themselves to be in competition with choral music teachers, and vice versa. Not only do the two factions fail to work together, but occasionally the teacher of one group belittles the other in an attempt to build up his or her group. Such friction undermines the total music program and is a waste of emotional energy for the teachers, to say nothing about its unethical qualities.

Music teachers sometimes overlook the school clerical and custodial staff, or they feel superior to them and let those feelings show. A successful music program depends on the assistance of the nonteaching staff, but thoughtless music teachers occasionally take this help for granted and fail to acknowledge it in any way.

Music teachers need to take an active interest in school activities. They cannot say on the one hand that music is an integral part of the curriculum and then shy away from serving on schoolwide curriculum committees because they feel that music is a "special" area. Nor should they display little interest in the fate of the football team or the winter play, especially if they want the support of the physical education and theater departments for the music program.

Music Teaching and You

It is fine to talk in general about the qualities a good music teacher should possess. But there must be more than talk. The time comes when you need to look at yourself in terms of those desirable characteristics. Self-evaluation is not an easy thing to do. One is torn between being too kind and being too tough on oneself. Even if the self-evaluation isn't perfect, the effort will be revealing and informative. As a result, you will understand yourself a bit better than you did before, especially in terms of being a teacher.

A form is provided (see Figure 3.1) to guide you in the process. Please complete the form, even if you never show it to anyone.

Questions
1. Think of two good school music teachers you have had and of two who you think were not so good. What in their personalities and teaching methods made them either successful or unsuccessful?

2. Think of a community that you know well. If there are professional musicians in it, what efforts are made to promote coordinated efforts between them and the school music teachers? What is the relationship between the private music teachers and the school music teachers? Between the music teachers and the music merchants?

3. What are the most important qualities for a successful music teacher?

4. Why should you avoid trying to imitate the actions or characteristics of a particular teacher you admire?

References   Ausubel, D. P., Novak, J. D., & Hanesian, H. (1978). *Educational psychology* (2nd ed.). New York: Holt, Rinehart & Winston.

Brenton, M. (1970). *What's happened to teacher?* New York: Avon Books.

Klotman, R. H. (Ed.). (1972). *Teacher education in music: Final report.* Reston, VA: Music Educators National Conference.

CHAPTER 4

Preparing to Be a Teacher

*C*hapter 5 describes the first step in preparing to be a music teacher: adopting the attitude that you are entering the profession of music education. This chapter deals more with the actual preparation in terms of courses and other activities.

In one sense, you don't need to think about the content of the program you must follow to become certified as a music teacher. The state in which you attend college and your university or college have already decided that for you. However, you will get much more out of your college experiences if you understand the reasons for the various requirements and how this course or that requirement contributes to preparing you to be a successful music teacher.

SPECIFIC OR GENERAL PREPARATION?

It would be nice if everyone knew now the exact job that he or she were going to hold a few years from now after graduation. Knowing that, the faculty and textbook writers could prescribe exactly what each future teacher needed to know and be able to do in order to succeed in a particular job. Unfortunately, this is not possible. Instead, the best that college instructors and textbook writers can do is to provide some guidelines and suggestions that work in a majority of situations.

While that may not seem very impressive to you now, please take advantage of whatever help anyone offers. Many a college student who had major doubts about what she or he was learning in music methods classes has discovered, once out in the real world of teaching, that the materials studied years before (and, it is hoped, still available in the teacher's personal professional library) are real lifesavers.

The fact that no one can know where or what area of music you will teach means you will probably study some things in music methods courses that you don't think you will need. For example, you may intend to be a high school band director, but find you have to learn something about teaching music to children in the elementary schools. Or you may be a singer who never intends to touch an instrument other than piano. In either case you may find yourself responsible for a class or two in elementary school general music or leading an ensemble of instruments while it accompanies a choral group. Beginning teachers, especially, are more likely to work in small schools in which versatility is crucial. The more attractive and specialized positions are usually filled with experienced teachers.

There is another reason for a broad undergraduate preparation. Suppose that it could be determined just what you needed to know to be a music teacher, and you were given only those courses. That situation would be like buying only the amount of blanket needed to cover you at night. You would like on your back with your hands at your side as your tailored blanket pattern was traced and then cut. Yes, this procedure would save blanket material, but a problem would come up if you wanted to change positions as you slept, because you would have no cover for any other position. A narrow teacher education program provides little "cover" for different positions in music education and inhibits growth in the profession. As an undergraduate it is impossible to be able to predict exactly what will be useful to you ten or twenty years from now.

The concept of preparing music teachers for all grades, kindergarten through grade 12, is certainly justified. The vast majority of jobs available to music teachers involve teaching on more than one level.

APPLYING MUSICAL KNOWLEDGE AND SKILLS

Good music teachers must also be good musicians. While they may not play their instruments or sing quite as well as someone who concentrated on that aspect of music (although it is not at all unusual for some music education students to perform as well as or better than performance majors), they must know music well. Why? A person can't teach what he or she does not know. In addition to knowing music themselves, they must know it so well that they can teach it to someone else, which is no easy accomplishment.

Several areas are especially important to future music teachers. One is aural skills. The ear training you receive in college is invaluable to you in teaching music. Persons who are unable to hear what is happening in a musical work can never be successful music teachers. Although that statement may seem exaggerated, it is not. Music is an aural art, and aural perception and comprehension are essential in teaching it. Teachers of general music classes in elementary schools need to be able to hear wrong notes and faulty intonation; such skills are not the exclusive province of ensemble directors.

A knowledge of music history and literature is also necessary. Music teachers select music, which involves a knowledge of musical works, and they then inform students about the music. Therefore, they need to be knowledgeable about the world of music. And the word *world* is appropriate here. In a time of instant communication and jet airplanes as well as the large immigrations of people to America from every area of the world, a knowledge of more than the traditional art and folk music of Western civilization is imperative.

What you learn in applied music instruction is also vital to becoming a successful music teacher. True, you are not going to play many trumpet or saxophone solos or sing arias for your classes, but you are going to teach them about phrases, articulations, and projecting feelings in songs. These are points that require an internal understanding that comes from experiences involving performing phrases, articulations, and projecting the message of a vocal work. Such points seem to defy verbal explanations.

Learning in Music Education Courses

What should you be learning in a course that introduces you to the field of music education? That seems simple enough: introductory information about music education. But there is more to it than that, because music education—and your future involvement with it—includes a number of different topics:

- the reasons why teaching music is important;
- the nature of the teaching process;
- the nature of learning in music and music education;
- the qualifications and characteristics of persons who teach music; and
- the nature of the profession of music education, including its development and features.

Some of the information you are expected to learn in education courses is somewhat different from what you usually encounter in college courses. In music theory classes you acquire skills in listening and learn about the function of various chords. In music history you study musical works and the development of music. Much of this type of information was unknown to you before you took those courses. That is only partly true of music education courses, in which information is occasionally presented that appears to be as novel as, "The sun rises in the east."

Why is information sometimes included in music education courses and this book that you may already know? Why doesn't the instructor or author assume that as previous or existing knowledge and move on to the new stuff? There are at least four reasons for including some information that may not appear to be entirely new.

1. Some students in the course do not know or have not thought about the topic being discussed. Not every student starts at the same place in terms of what he or she knows. It is better for an instructor or textbook to be thorough than to omit points that some students need.

2. The "I-knew-it-all-along" phenomenon is probably operating on some of the information that was thought to have been known. Social psychologists have repeatedly discovered that people often think that they already knew something that later became known to them. Humans have a strong tendency to look back at a situation and to believe that its outcome was obvious, commonsense, and something they could have predicted at the time. In fact, contradictory proverbs are readily available to help people declare the accuracy of their hindsight: "Absence makes the heart grow fonder" versus "Out of sight, out of mind," "Haste makes waste" versus "He who hesitates is lost," and on and on. As the great Danish philosopher-theologian Søren Kierkegaard concluded, "Life is lived forwards, but understood backwards."

3. Sometimes all of us need reminders or need to have our attention focused on something that we could have figured out for ourselves, *if* we had taken the time to think about it carefully. All of us, if we took the time, "know" that a teacher should maintain eye contact when teaching a class or group and that a variety of activities is more stimulating for most students than grinding away for most of a class or rehearsal on a single topic or activity. Yet, unless reminded (and even after being reminded, in some cases), beginning teachers (and some experienced ones, too!) will ignore these and other commonsense facts that they already "knew." Part of what a music education course can do is raise one's consciousness about what may seem simple and obvious. So, once in a while it may be really helpful to remind teachers that "the sun rises in the east."

4. Usually (but not always) phenomena involving human behavior are *partly* known. If you observe life systematically and carefully, you will learn quite a bit of what social scientists have uncovered in their research. This should not be surprising, because indeed it would be illogical to have important information about how human beings act remain totally hidden, only to be uncovered by researchers. Important new information about human behavior rarely comes "out of a clear blue sky." For example, the fact that the use of heavy doses of criticism is not the best means of motivating people was probably apparent to most people before that fact was confirmed by research studies.

So, what is the value of research on such topics? Research studies are conducted systematically, sometimes under controlled circumstances, and are therefore more precise and verifiable than the more casual impressions of individuals. And every so often, the unexpected happens; occasionally the results of research studies involving human behavior do not confirm common sense, or at least they clarify common sense.

Learning in music education courses consists partly of gaining new information, partly of carefully thinking about the process of teaching, and partly of looking at the teaching of music and those who do it in a way that contributes to a better understanding of what teaching music is all about.

Knowledge of Teaching Techniques

Good teachers know how to teach what their students are to learn. For example, if a band plays a passage in a staccato style, how does the teacher get the idea of staccato over to the players so that they can execute it correctly? Without knowing how to do this, the teacher must resort to pleading, "Now, make those notes *short!*" This procedure is all right as a beginning, but experienced teachers know that just telling the students to play short notes is not enough to teach staccato, except for a few short notes that might happen by trial and error.

Teachers should have in mind numerous examples, analogies, and explanations for use in teaching. They cannot stop a class, run to their desks, and thumb through a book to find this technique or that bit of information. Whenever possible, music teachers should anticipate the problems that might be encountered in a certain piece. If a work requires staccato playing, they can review various ideas for playing staccato (it's not the same on every instrument) prior to presenting the piece to the group.

In teaching a performing group, teachers should teach their students to do more than execute the printed music symbols and follow the conductor's gestures. Singing and playing can easily become mechanical, so that the students make music in a parrotlike fashion without any understanding of what they are doing. Playing and singing are fine, but they are only a part of music education. Students should also be taught something about the style, harmony, form, rhythmic structure, and composers of the more substantial works the group performs.

Preprofessional Experiences

Observations. Many states and colleges require that future teachers have contacts with schools and students prior to the student-teaching experience. These contacts are called by a variety of names, with "field experiences" perhaps being the one most commonly used. The purpose of field experiences is to encourage future teachers to think about and be aware of school situations well before the last semester of the undergraduate preparation, when student teaching is usually taken. In fact, some colleges and states specify contacts with schools beginning in the freshman year, and sometimes the observation of disabled or minority students is also stipulated.

Usually field experiences take place in a variety of school situations so that future teachers gain a perspective of the total music curriculum. Many of them are for one time only in any one school or with any one teacher. Occasionally a small-project type of teaching is done in conjunction with a music methods class, such as when a committee of three students develops and teaches a lesson on playing the autoharp to a third grade classroom.

The usefulness of these pre-student-teaching experiences depends to a great extent on the attitude of the future teachers. If they look upon them as just putting in time to fulfill a requirement, then they probably will receive the minimum benefit from them. On the other hand, if they go into school situations and try to analyze the teaching process (*not* the teacher as a person) and learn from what they see, they can benefit a great deal from these experiences.

And what should future teachers attempt to analyze as they observe school music classes? The teaching process as described in Chapter 2. (Surprised?) Because these experiences present only a limited time to observe a teacher, and because there is an ethical question about future teachers attempting in an hour or two to guess the motivation of a teacher, the five questions presented in that chapter should probably be reduced to four for purposes of the observation experiences. For each class, then, the observing students should answer these questions.

1. What was the teacher trying to have the students learn?
2. What methods did the teacher employ to help the students learn?
3. What appeared to be the musical background and abilities of the students?
4. What were the observable results of the instruction?

In addition, student observers will find it useful to notice how the teacher managed some of the routine matters of teaching. Such matters include the setup of the room, the distribution of music, the promptness with which the class is started and conducted, the assignment of seats for the students, and the manner in which attendance is taken. In no sense are such actions equal in importance to the amount of learning that takes place, but they can affect the educational results and are therefore worth observing.

Student Teaching. Student teaching has three purposes. First, it provides the future teacher with the opportunity to observe and work with an established, successful teacher. A student teacher in a real sense is an apprentice to an experienced teacher. This apprenticeship permits an intensive observation and testing experience that is considered essential in all teacher education programs. The cooperating teachers (the term often assigned to such teachers) are selected because they are considered to be better than average. The cooperating teacher accepts student teachers largely out of a sense of professional commitment, not to make his or her job easier or to gain extra income.*

The second purpose of student teaching is to provide a guided induction into teaching. Student teachers can move step-by-step into situations structured by cooperating teachers; consequently, student teachers are not just pushed into jobs in which they must either sink or swim.

The third purpose of student teaching is to establish the fact that the student teacher can in fact teach. A prospective employer wants to know, "How did this person do when in front of a classroom?" A good college record and good character recommendations are fine, but there is no better test of teaching ability than actually teaching in a "real life" situation.

It helps if you are clear on what everyone's role is in the student-teaching situation. Your role as student teacher has already been pointed out: an apprentice. It is an in-between situation. You will be a teacher, but yet not quite. You will be closer in age to the students than their teacher, but you are expected to act like a teacher, not a student or an intermediary between the class and the teacher. The students know that you are a student teacher and that after a while you won't be around anymore. They also suspect that you won't have a lot to say about their final grades or their seats in the clarinet section. In a real sense, the position of student teacher is one of a "guest" or "temporary resident." You will be working with someone else's classes in a school in which you are not a permanent employee. You will not be in a position to make significant decisions without the

---

*The stipend for supervising a student teacher is only a token payment, if there is any at all.

approval of the cooperating teacher, to fill out requisitions unless the supervising teacher approves them, or to negotiate a different schedule for music classes.

Yet you will be a teacher. By that time you will have had much specialized training for what you are doing. Your role will be that of teacher, and you will be expected to show up promptly each day school is in session. You will be allowed some initiative in what is taught, but such undertakings should be cleared with the cooperating teacher ahead of time.

The role of a cooperating teacher is that of mentor to the student teacher. A mentor is one who guides, offers constructive help, and answers questions. Offering suggestions for improvement is part of that process, as are commendations for work that is done well. Student teachers need not agree with every suggestion they receive, but the cooperating teachers' thoughts should be given careful consideration and, in most cases, given a try. In addition, the cooperating teacher is responsible for a report to the college about your teaching and usually is asked to write a letter of recommendation. For all of these reasons the usefulness of the student-teaching experience depends very much on the cooperating teacher.

College supervisors usually do not have a major role in the student-teaching situation. This situation is so for one simple reason: The number of times they can visit a student teacher is usually limited. Even if three to five visits are possible, these usually last for only a couple of classes. The college supervisor's role consists more of making the initial placement and then serving as a coordinator between the college and the cooperating teacher. If important problems arise in the student-teaching situation, then the college supervisor's role becomes very significant. Also, if a college supervisor has observed your teaching, he or she can write a letter of recommendation for you that is more credible than letters from other professors because it can report on your teaching.

The amount and type of teaching that a student teacher undertakes depends on the cooperating teacher's opinion of the particular needs of the program. Usually the first week or so is spent observing and learning about the situation. Gradually the student teacher is given more responsibility. Often this initial responsibility consists of working with individuals or small groups and doing menial chores such as passing out books, moving chairs, and typing tests. After a while the student teacher is given entire classes and eventually most of the cooperating teacher's schedule.

For student teachers who demonstrate initiative, optimism, and a willingness to learn, the student teacher experience is most rewarding.

CONTINUED GROWTH AND SELF-EVALUATION

Although it seems like a long way off, you should realize that continued growth as a teacher is both desired and expected. If you graduate from college at the age of twenty-two, you have forty-three years remaining before you reach the age of sixty-five, which is the most common retirement age for school teachers. Think of it, forty-three years! This is a very long time just to think about, but it is an even longer time to remain fresh, vital, and interesting. Without continued growth, teachers run the risk of repeating one year's experience forty-three times rather than improving with each year of experience. No one should want to be "in a rut" for an entire career.

What can teachers do to continue growing professionally? The most obvious means, and one required in most states before permanent certification can be attained, is to continue study at the graduate level during summers or evenings.

Professional associations, especially MENC, are another means of continuing to grow as a teacher. Its in-service activities and Professional Certification Program are described in Chapter 5.

Other means of professional growth include the reading of journals and their reports of research. Teachers should be aware of the results of studies of music teaching and of practices in music education. Research results are reported at MENC meetings and in its publications. Music teachers should not be satisfied with answering the question "Does this teaching procedure work?" In addition, they should ask, "Would another procedure work better?" Being satisfied with something just because it happens to work is like being content to spend a lifetime hopping about on one leg. Undoubtedly hopping works, but there is a more efficient way to get around; it's called walking.

Self-Improvement

Even after taking advantage of every opportunity and graduating from a good music education program, beginning teachers should realize that they must still teach themselves to teach well. No course or series of courses, no professor, no book, no college can impart enough information about the particular school, its students, and its unique nature to train teachers fully for the job they will undertake. Teachers finally must succeed or fail on their own. They must look objectively at themselves and improve on their own work.

Although self-evaluation has the obvious disadvantage of being somewhat subjective, it is the only practical means open to most music teachers. For one thing, self-evaluation is a continuous process. It is not something that occurs once or twice a semester; it should go on in one form or another during every class. For another thing, it is done with full knowledge of what one is trying to teach and of the total school situation.

Evaluations by outsiders are of limited usefulness. School administrators seldom know much about music. Visits by school principals to classrooms often bring forth comments about things other than the learning of music—"The students seemed to enjoy the class" and similar statements. Even adjudicators at contests, who are competent in music, are listening to the performance of a few prepared works with no knowledge of the school situation. School music supervisors can offer the best critiques for teachers. However, their time available for such work is limited, and many school districts do not have music supervisors.

Teacher Rating Forms

The use of forms by which students evaluate teachers is standard at the college level for professors seeking promotion or tenure, but such forms are seldom used in the schools. Even at the college level, rating forms are of limited value. The ratings given are only partly the result of the instructor's actions. For example, instructors of required classes for freshmen and sophomores seldom rate as high as do instructors of junior- and senior-level courses in the students' major area. Rating forms seem to work best with mature students; they are of little worth in elementary and middle schools. The other problem with teacher rating forms is that the responses must be only general reactions about the teacher. A general statement that one is or is not a good teacher is not very helpful in improving instruction.

Playback of Classes

Another specific means of self-evaluation is the use of a videotape or tape recorder. Some teachers make a recording of their classes or rehearsals, which they then analyze. The recordings serve two purposes. They allow a more leisurely and thoughtful study of what the class has done, and they enable teachers to evaluate their own efforts in teaching the class or rehearsal. In analyzing a tape for self-evaluation purposes, teachers can ask themselves questions such as the following.

1. Were there unnecessary delays and wasted time?
2. Were the points on which I corrected the group those that needed attention?
3. Did my suggestions to the group result in improvements?
4. Were my statements clear and decisive?
5. Was my conducting clear and decisive?
6. Did I repeat certain words and phrases—such as "OK?," "You know," "Right"—so frequently that they became annoying?
7. Was the pace of the class about right?
8. Were there relaxing breaks in the rehearsal or class routine—a little humor or something done just for the pleasure of it?
9. Specifically, what was accomplished in the class?
10. Did I encourage the students to discover and learn some points for themselves, or did I direct every action?

No one has ever achieved the status of "perfect teacher." Teachers are human. However, each teacher's unique strengths and weaknesses give him or her a distinctive way of teaching. Such individuality is desirable and can be developed along with the requisites of sensitive musicianship and personal maturity. Music teachers need to relate their educational efforts to the efforts of other professionals in music and in education. Finally, teachers must look objectively at their work throughout their careers if they are to achieve their potential as teachers of music.

Questions

1. Why isn't it useful to write or suggest very specific "cookbook"-like directions for teaching certain aspects of music?

2. Why do music teachers need to be good musicians themselves?

3. Why should music teachers today know more than the traditional art and folk music of Western civilization?

4. What examples, in addition to getting a group to play short notes, can you describe that demonstrate a music teacher's knowledge of teaching techniques?

5. What are the main reasons for requiring future teachers to observe classes and begin participation in teaching even before student teaching?

6. In the student-teaching situation,
   a. what is the role of the student teacher?
   b. what is the role of the cooperating teacher in the schools?
   c. what is the role of the college supervisor?

7. Why is it so important for music teachers to continue to grow professionally throughout their entire careers?

8. What are some ways in which music teachers can continue to grow professionally after graduation from college?

Project

Think of three different things that you have learned in music theory or music history in the last three weeks. Then decide how each of those things will help you in being a good music teacher. Share your thinking with your music education class.

CHAPTER 5

The Music Education Profession

Music teachers are never completely alone in their work, even though they may be the only teacher of music in a particular school. They are identified as a "music teacher," whether they like it or not. Their work is affected to some degree by what others who teach music have done in the past and are doing now. This happens in several ways.

To begin with, teachers usually succeed other music teachers, and so they inherit a legacy from their predecessors. If, for example, the previous choral teacher devoted his or her main efforts to a big musical each year, the students and community may expect an annual spring musical gala.

Another influence is that administrators and teachers are aware of what goes on in neighboring school districts, and they tend to make comparisons among school music programs. There is an unfortunate tendency on the part of some school board members and administrators to be guided more by what similar schools are doing than by what is best for their particular situation. Too often they ask questions such as "Why should we start a string program (add more classes of general music, buy some quality instruments for music in the elementary classrooms—the same sentiment can be applied to many matters) when Sturgis and Hillsdale don't have one?"

Also, all school music teachers are involved in the same general type of work. The same conditions and public attitudes affect everyone who teaches music in the schools. If a school music program succeeds, music education in general benefits. And, unfortunately, every music teacher or program that fails hurts music education a little bit.

WHAT IS A PROFESSION?

Music education is often spoken of as a profession, but is it? What characteristics should a type of work possess in order to earn the distinction of being a "profession"? Four factors seem essential for a profession.

One characteristic is that the work of a profession requires extensive education and preparation, usually a baccalaureate degree from college and often several years of additional study. A medical doctor graduates from college and completes three or four years of medical school plus several more years of residency. Music teachers do not have quite as much training, but they usually hold a college degree plus at least one year of graduate study. So they qualify in terms of amount of education.

A second characteristic of a profession is the responsibility for making decisions. An architect plans—makes decisions about—the design and construction of a building; electricians, plumbers, bricklayers, and other workers carry out specific tasks according to the blueprints of the architect. Music teachers make decisions about how and what students learn in music classes, but they are usually also responsible for carrying them out. Nevertheless, they do make decisions about the content of what they teach and the method they use to teach it.

A third characteristic of a profession is the commitment to the work shared by the membership. Most professionals do not think of their jobs as only nine-to-five tasks. They work more than the minimum number of hours, and they work when no one tells them to do so. It is not unusual for them to take work home with them. Most music teachers (but not all!) are committed to their profession. In fact, their deep sense of commitment sometimes causes problems for them if the public and school administrators do not view the teacher's work as particularly important and do not support it well. That situation can cause frustration and conflict.

Finally, a profession has an organization that is mainly concerned with the advancement of the profession, not with the welfare of its members. This is the main difference between a union and a professional association. A union's main obligation is to improve the pay and working conditions of its members; a professional organization seeks to keep its members current on developments in the field and to provide for their continued growth in carrying out their work. This is not to say that unions are wrong or bad (because they have an important role in society) but only that the nature of a professional association is different.

The Music Educators National Conference

The professional organization of school music teachers in the United States is the Music Educators National Conference. It consists of the national organization and fifty-three state-federated units. It works to advance music education in a number of ways. One is the in-service education of its members. This continuing education is accomplished through conferences and the publication of books, audio- and videotapes, and journals. The *Music Educators Journal* is its main vehicle of communication of professional ideas, but its list of serial publications includes research and other specialized areas. All state units also publish magazines. This aspect of MENC's efforts seeks to help music teachers do what they do better.

The MENC Professional Certification Program promotes and recognizes quality teaching and teachers. It gives visibility to teachers with eight or more years of experience who have demonstrated continuing professional growth and successful teaching. Its purpose is to supplement the state-licensing requirements of music teachers, which usually require only a low minimum in terms of preparation to teach and of continued study after employment. Like certification programs in medicine, architecture, and many other fields, the MENC Professional Certification Program is not a function of any governmental agency, so it carries no requirements for school boards. However, as do the certification programs of other professional organizations, MENC identifies individuals who have attained certain levels of training and competency in the field. Such recognition will very likely have some long-range benefits for those individuals in terms of job placement and salary, as well as increased professional status.

A second way MENC seeks to advance music education is its efforts to inform others—school administrators and board members, parents, elected officials, and the general public—about the values and nature of music education. These efforts include Music in Our Schools Month, along with its nationally televised concert, pamphlets, radio and television spot announcements, and cooperative efforts with other groups interested in promoting music and music study. These outreach efforts also include contacting governmental leaders and agencies to inform them about the particular needs of music education. Because the health of school music programs depends on the support of others, informing people about music education is a very important topic.

A third way MENC seeks to advance music education is by serving as the "conscience" of the profession. Although such a role is not an easy or a popular one, it is vital if the music education profession is to be effective and respected. Some person or some organization must encourage music teachers to look at themselves and their work in an objective, analytical way to see how it affects students and the image it presents the general public. MENC seeks to encourage music teachers to do the right things, not just to do things well.

To the degree that MENC is successful in promoting music education, all music teachers and students benefit. And the success of MENC depends on how well music teachers are united in supporting it. Smaller specialized groups within music education, such as choral directors and elementary music specialists in one method or another, cannot speak for music education as a whole. Teachers who are attracted to a specialized organization should still retain their commitment to and membership in MENC. If they do not, the profession becomes more fragmented and easier prey for the wolves of poor financial and administrative support. As Abraham Lincoln quoted from the Gospel of Mark, "A house divided against itself, that house cannot stand."

Being a Member of a Profession

How do you become a member of the music education profession? Fortunately, you do not have to wait until you have a job as a music teacher. In fact, the securing of a job, as important as that is, is only one step in the process. The first step can be taken now, and it is the most important one: *Begin thinking of yourself as a professional music educator.* Being a member of a profession is partly a matter of attitude, of the way you think about your work and preparation for that work. And that way of thinking is closely related to the characteristics of a profession presented a few pages back in this chapter. For one, it means securing the education necessary to become a music teacher. But more than that, it means viewing the music and music education courses you take as vital components of your professional preparation. Think of them as equipping you to make the right decisions about the music learning of the students when that time arrives.

Being a member of a profession means thinking about your work as more than a job, as more than something you must do to make a living. A professional person sees his or her work in a larger and more meaningful perspective. For example, teaching music is not just getting the students to sing some songs. Rather, it is using singing as a means of teaching music to students, which is something that will enrich their lives now and in the years to come. The difference between those two views of teaching songs to students may seem like hairsplitting, but it is not. It represents the essential difference between being employed and being professional.

People who think as professionals usually do certain things. One is that they join their professional organization, which in the case of music education is MENC. MENC sponsors collegiate groups designed specifically for bringing prospective music teachers into the profession. Collegiate Music Educators National Conference chapters (CMENC) are found in nearly 600 colleges and universities throughout the United States. The dues are about one-third those asked of teaching members, and yet student members receive all the benefits, including the *Music Educators Journal.*

Be active in your CMENC chapter. It offers a variety of activities and presentations that supplement the music methods courses. In addition, the contacts you make and the interest your participation demonstrates to future employers can be beneficial. If your CMENC chapter is not all that you think it should be, become active in it and make it better.

In addition to joining CMENC, you should begin reading the professional journals in music education. The articles in the *Music Educators Journal* are a good place to begin. A list of recommended articles from the journal is included at the end of this chapter. However, you should not stop there. Read also the magazines that cover your particular areas of interest, journals such as *General Music Today, The Choral Journal, The Instrumentalist,* and so on.

Try to attend a conference of music educators. While distance and expense may make attendance difficult, find out if such an experience might be possible. Registration fees at MENC conferences and those of its state units are greatly reduced for students members, and money can be saved by sharing rides and rooms. These events, especially the national conferences and those of medium- and large-sized states, are very impressive and professionally stimulating.

When it comes down to the bottom line, a profession is built by people. Music education and MENC are only nice abstractions unless people breathe life into them. Therefore, the quality of the music instruction students receive depends on the ability of the people who teach them music and their sense of professionalism about their work.

MUSIC TEACHERS AND THE COMMUNITY

There is more to being a music teacher than meeting classes and managing supplies and student grades. In addition to teaching, all music teachers must devote a small amount of time—perhaps one hour a week—to educating others about the purpose and values of music in the schools. Music educators understand the value of having music in the school curriculum, but most people do not. It is not that they don't want music in the schools; rather, it is that they are uninformed about its value in schools. Therefore when money is short, the support for music in the schools is "soft."

Furthermore, uninformed persons tend to look for the wrong things in forming opinions about the music program in their local schools. A win at a contest, even one of little importance, is often misconstrued as meaning that the schools have a fine total music program. In addition, almost all opinions are formed from hearing or seeing performance groups, which tends to put most of the attention on them. But these groups often involve only 10 or 15 percent of the student body. As a result, music for the other 85 percent of the students is largely forgotten.

What should music educators do to build better public understanding? The answer to that question depends on the situation and the teacher's abilities and interests. It may mean writing an annual report to the principal on the school's needs and plans in the area of music. It may mean making public performances more like "informances," in which an effort is made to educate the audience about music and music education. It may mean trying to get the band boosters to think of themselves as "music boosters" by supporting the addition of another teacher in orchestra and general music. It may mean taking time to work with the school guidance counselors to avoid scheduling conflicts. A more complete listing of ideas for informing others about music education is contained in the MENC publication *Beyond the Classroom: Informing Others*.

Part of the task of informing others about school music and developing their support lies in reaching particular groups of people in the community.

Professional Musicians

School music programs are affected by the other music activities and interests in the community. A city or town with an active musical life helps the school music program, and, in turn, effective school music programs contribute to the level of the arts in communities. For these reasons music educators should promote musical activities in the community. Also, music teachers should work to bring professional performers into the schools. To the extent possible, in-school performances by professional performers and the educational concerts should be jointly planned ventures between the school music teachers and the performers. The benefits are greater when such cooperation takes place.

Attempts have been made to define the "turf" or domain of professional musicians and of school groups. In 1947, MENC, the American Association of School Administrators, and the American Federation of Musicians drew up a comprehensive Music Code of Ethics (see Appendix B) that specifies which activities are the domain of school music groups and which should be left to professional musicians. The code has been reaffirmed every seven years since 1947. All music educators should be familiar with and abide by the provisions of the code.

Music Merchants

Contacts between music teachers and music merchants should also be conducted ethically. Because music teachers are employed by the public, and therefore should treat everyone equally, they should not accept personal favors or commissions from merchants. The acceptance of gratuities has a way of obligating the teacher and gives the appearance of favoritism. The choice of store and purchases made should be determined solely on the basis of the quality of goods and services in relation to the cost. When purchases amount to $100 or more, it is wise (and usually required by law or school regulation) that bids be secured. Competitive bidding encourages the best price from the merchants and provides proof that business transactions are handled fairly and openly.

In addition to maintaining ethical relationships, music teachers need to work with music merchants in effort to promote music in the schools. Clearly, it is in the interests of both parties to do so.

Private Music Teachers

Ethical relationships should also be maintained with private music teachers. Never should the work of an incompetent private teacher be deprecated publicly; that person should simply not be recommended. Whenever possible, music teachers should provide interested parents with the names of more than one competent private teacher.

The level of the school music program can be advanced considerably by the efforts of good private music teachers. This is especially important in the case of instrumental students who have progressed beyond intermediate levels. Because few instrumental teachers know the advanced techniques on more than one or two instruments, the progress of the school band or orchestra depends in part on the availability of private instruction.

Community Organizations

Community service clubs and organizations, and especially a local arts council, should not be ignored. Service clubs sometimes provide scholarship help to enable worthy students to study, and they also contribute travel monies on occasion. These groups also are a good means of getting information about the music program to the public. The arts council represents a ready-made group that supports the arts, and such support can be valuable if the music program faces financial cutbacks.

The Community

The most useful contacts music teachers have with the public are the parents of the students. Information should be supplied to the parents periodically about the activities and goals of the music program. Slide shows, videotapes, and brochures can be prepared explaining the program. In some instances, parent support groups have been of great help in furthering high school performing groups, especially bands. Over time, music teachers should steer the interests of such organizations toward the entire music program, not just one segment of it.

Parents look to music teachers for guidance when their child is contemplating a career in music. School guidance counselors may also be involved in such matters, but their knowledge about music is usually limited. To assist students who are considering music teaching and other music careers, MENC has prepared materials on careers in music.

TEACHERS AND EDUCATIONAL GOALS

Teachers have both opportunities and limitations in determining the goals in public education. They must accept the broad goals endorsed by society and the educational system. Teachers who act contrary to these goals reduce the total effectiveness of the schools, to say nothing of possibly losing their jobs. For instance, teachers cannot ignore the many for the benefit of the few or teach the violent overthrow of the government without detracting from the results the schools seek to achieve. These broad mandates apply to music teachers just as much as they do to other teachers. Music is a specialized area of study, but so are other school subjects.

The educational mandates guiding teachers are broad and general. They are something like the directions a passenger gives a taxi driver. The rider gives the destination, but decisions about the best way to get there are the driver's, because he or she is the "expert" in getting around that city. There are some general restrictions, such as not hitting other cars and not driving on the sidewalk, that the passenger doesn't need to state specifically. Taxi drivers, like teachers, make the detailed decisions about the process of reaching the destination and implement them as intelligently and efficiently as possible.

Who finally decides what the specific objectives are for music classes—administrators, boards of education, governmental agencies, or teachers? The forces that affect educational goals and objectives are diverse and often conflicting. States authorize local school boards to oversee education, and school boards then employ administrators to guide the daily efforts of education. But the matter does not stop there. Teachers can also influence decisions within school systems. Because administrators rarely know as much about each subject matter area as the teachers who are specialized in an area, they must depend on the music faculty members for guidance and leadership concerning the music program. Then after considering the other needs in the school system, they will try to render fair and equitable decisions about how fully the recommendations of the music teachers can be implemented. Unless administrators are informed by the music faculty members about what is needed, they will assume that the present situation is satisfactory and will tend to continue it.

The detailed, within-class decisions are the responsibility of each teacher. There is no way for administrators to oversee such matters. There simply isn't time for them to look over the shoulder of every teacher, and (except for music supervisors) they lack the knowledge of music to make specialized decisions. Very few school administrators know the correct embouchure for the French horn or what the Kodály-Curwen hand signs are!

Because the understanding and support of school administrators and school boards is such a critical matter in the fate of school music programs, their understanding and support is essential. For this reason, informing them is a necessary part of all music educators' work. This topic is discussed in Chapter 10.

Questions

1. What are the four main characteristics of a profession?

2. What are the differences between a professional association and a union?

3. In what ways does MENC attempt to advance music education?

4. How can thinking of yourself as a professional music educator influence your outlook toward
    a. the music and music education courses you take,
    b. the teaching of music to students,
    c. participation in your CMENC chapter, and
    d. the articles and books you read?

5. In what ways can music educators and professional musicians work together?

6. In what ways do private music teachers benefit the school music program?

7. Do music teachers influence the goals of the school music program? In what ways?

Project   Select two articles from the *Music Educators Journal* written in recent years (for examples, see the Suggested Readings section). Using the form on page 63, report on each article. Make a copy of the form for your second report.

ARTICLE REPORT FORM

Title of article:
Author:
Magazine or journal:
Date of publication:

Main point of article:

Subpoints in article:

Applications of points to music education:

Suggested
Readings

The following suggested readings are all articles from the *Music Educators Journal*. Read as many of them as possible. They will contribute to your knowledge of your profession, and you can use two of them to help you complete the project for this chapter.

Anderson, W. M. (1991). Toward a multicultural future. *Music Educators Journal, 77*(9), 29.

Andress, B. (1989). Music for every stage. *Music Educators Journal, 76*(2), 22.

Austin, J. R. (1990). Competition: Is music education the loser? *Music Educators Journal, 76*(6), 21.

Balkin, A. (1990). What is creativity? What is it not? *Music Educators Journal, 76*(9), 29.

Battisti, F. L. (1989). Clarifying priorities for the high school band. *Music Educators Journal, 76*(1), 23.

Boyle, J. D. (1989). Perspective on evaluation. *Music Educators Journal, 76*(4), 23.

Brand, M. (1990). Master music teachers: What makes them great. *Music Educators Journal, 77*(2), 22.

Byo, J. (1990). Teach your instrumental students to listen. *Music Educators Journal, 77*(4), 43.

Cassidy, J. W. (1990). Managing the mainstreamed classroom. *Music Educators Journal, 76*(8), 40.

Colwell, R. (1990). Research findings: Shake well before using. *Music Educators Journal, 77*(3), 29.

Curtis, M. V. (1988). Understanding the black aesthetic experience. *Music Educators Journal, 75*(2), 23.

Cutietta, R. A. (1991) Popular music: An ongoing challenge. *Music Educators Journal, 77*(8), 26.

Delzell, J. K. (1987). Time management for quality teaching. *Music Educators Journal, 73*(8), 43.

Delzell, J. K. (1988). Guidelines for a balanced performance schedule. *Music Educators Journal, 74*(8), 34.

DeNicola, D. N. (1989). MENC goes to college. *Music Educators Journal, 75*(5), 35.

Dodson, T. (1989). Are students learning music in band? *Music Educators Journal, 76*(3), 25.

Eisner, E. W. (1987). Educating the whole person: Arts in the curriculum. *Music Educators Journal, 73*(8), 37.

Fisher, R. E. (1991). Personal skills: Passport to effective teaching. *Music Educators Journal, 77*(6), 21.

Fox, D. B. (1991). Music, development, and the young child. *Music Educators Journal, 77*(5), 42.

Fox, G. C. (1990). Making music festivals work. *Music Educators Journal, 76*(7), 59.

Gerber, T. (1989). Reaching all students: The ultimate challenge. *Music Educators Journal, 75*(7), 37.

Herman, S. (1988). Unlocking the potential of junior high choirs. *Music Educators Journal, 75*(4), 33.

Hoffer, C. R. (1986). Standards in music education. *Music Educators Journal, 72*(10), 58.

Hoffer, C. R. (1987). Tomorrow's directions in the education of music teachers. *Music Educators Journal, 73*(6), 27.

Hoffer, C. R. (1988). Informing others about music education. *Music Educators Journal, 74*(8), 30.

Hoffer, C. R. (1989). A new frontier. *Music Educators Journal, 75*(7), 34.

Hoffer, C. R. (1990). The two halves of music in the schools. *Music Educators Journal, 76*(7), 96.

Hughes, W. O. (1987). The next challenge: High school general music. *Music Educators Journal, 73*(8), 33.

Johnson, E. L., & Johnson, M. D. (1989). Planning + effort = a year of success. *Music Educators Journal, 75*(6), 40.

Kratus, J. (1990). Structuring the music curriculum for creative learning. *Music Educators Journal, 76*(9), 33.

Kuzmich, J. (1989). New styles, new technologies, new possibilities in jazz. *Music Educators Journal, 76*(3), 41.

Kuzmich, J. (1991). Popular music in your program: Growing with the times. *Music Educators Journal, 77*(8), 50.

McCoy, C. W. (1989). Basic training: Working with inexperienced choirs. *Music Educators Journal, 75*(8), 43.

Merrion, M. (1990). How master teachers handle discipline. *Music Educators Journal, 77*(2), 26.

Moore, J. L. S. (1990). Strategies for fostering creative thinking. *Music Educators Journal, 76*(9), 38.

Music Educators Journal. (1988). [Sesquicentennial issue]. *74*(6).

Phillips, K. H. (1988). Choral music comes of age. *Music Educators Journal, 75*(4), 23.

Radocy, R. E. (1989). Evaluating student achievement. *Music Educators Journal, 76*(4), 30.

Shehan, P. K. (1987). Finding a national music style: Listen to the children. *Music Educators Journal, 73*(9), 39.

Shuler, S. C. (1990). Solving instructional problems through research. *Music Educators Journal, 77*(3), 35.

Sims, W. L. (1990). Sound approaches to elementary music listening. *Music Educators Journal, 77*(4), 38.

Small, A. R. (1987). Music teaching and critical thinking. *Music Educators Journal, 74*(1), 46.

Stockton, J. L. (1987). Insights from a master Japanese teacher. *Music Educators Journal, 73*(6), 27.

Thompson, K. (1990). Working toward solutions in mainstreaming. *Music Educators Journal, 76*(8), 31.

Von Seggen, M. (1990), Magnet music programs. *Music Educators Journal, 76*(7), 50.

Webster, P. R. (1990). Creativity and creative thinking. *Music Educators Journal, 77*(9), 22.

Wenner, G. C. (1988). Joining forces with the arts community. *Music Educators Journal, 75*(4), 46.

CHAPTER 6

The Content of Music Classes

Vito Amata takes his band through a series of warm-up exercises. The students play several B-flat concert scales, each in a different rhythmic pattern. Then other keys are added to the routine. Next, he has the band play through some of the music in the folders. Vito almost never stops the band because they have had the music for some time now and a performance is coming up in the near future. Nothing in the warm-up exercises is mentioned again in the rehearsal.

Sharonda Billups has her middle school general music class figure out the words spelled by patterns of notes in the treble and bass clefs. The students study the notes on the sheets she has given them. Then they write the letters for a word like cabbage *below the notes when they see those notes in the notation.*

What did the students in Vito's and in Sharonda's classes learn? What do students learn from just playing through some music or only naming notes? What did Vito's students learn from the warm-up routines that did not relate to any of the music played in the rehearsal?

Such questions get right to the heart of music teaching, because learning in music classes is what it is all about, as Chapter 1 pointed out. Just gathering students together in a class and calling it *music* does not ensure that music learning will actually happen. Music teachers, therefore, need to think carefully about the "stuff" that they are trying to teach. They need to be sure that it is significant in terms of music and that it is useful and meaningful to the students.

Sounds simple enough? Unfortunately, it isn't. Part of the value of the content of a music class is determined by what precedes and what follows it. Naming notes in Sharonda Billups' class will be useful if it is associated with musical sounds.

Otherwise, the activity is not of much more value than working crossword puzzles with music symbols and words. Playing scales in Vito Amata's rehearsal and running through works in the folders isn't very worthwhile, unless the goal is the conditioning of embouchures and the exercising of fingers.

Understanding subject matter content of a music class or rehearsal requires digging below the surface. It involves asking the hard but important questions about music teaching.

LEARNING IN MUSIC

The chorus at Middlebury High School is singing the Shaker song "Simple Gifts." What should the students be learning from singing this beautiful song? At least five things:

1. patterns of musical sounds—the syntax of music;
2. the song as a work of music;
3. understandings about musical processes and organization;

67

4. skills in performing and listening to music; and

5. attitudes about the particular piece and about music in general.

Each of these five outcomes of learning merits further discussion.

Musical Syntax

If music is organized sound, as it was defined in Chapter 2, then a sense of organization and patterns of sounds is absolutely required for a person to hear the sounds as music. Otherwise, they are just a random jumble, as when a cat walks on the keys of a piano.

The analogy between language and music is not a perfect one, but in a number of ways they are much alike. When learning language, children find out that "runs big slowly dog black the" is not an understandable pattern. They need similar learning in music, except with musical sounds, of course. Apparently a sense of patterns or syntax in language, and probably in music as well, is developed through experience with speaking and listening. Children enter school with several years' experience in hearing and speaking words. Then only after they have had much practice and experience with spoken language are they given the visual symbols for the words they already know aurally.

There is another similarity between language and music. Research studies indicate that the learning of syntax and the pronunciation of words develop early in life (Penfield & Roberts, 1959). By the time a child is ten years old, the ability for such learning begins to decrease. For this reason it is very important that children in the primary grades of elementary school be given many opportunities for gaining a sense of musical syntax and learning to be accurate in singing pitch.

The syntax of music is probably the first type of learning that students should acquire in music, because without it the other four areas of learning won't mean much. Syntax alone can carry a person quite a distance in the world of music. For example, most of the early jazz musicians had little formal training and could not read music, yet their great intuitive sense for musical patterns more than compensated for these limitations. However, they were limited in what they knew about music, and music educators would not want their students today to be similarly restricted in what they know and can do in music.

Musical Works

The amount of music created throughout the world over the past couple of thousand years is huge beyond comprehension. Not only is there art music ranging from the 3800 works by Telemann to the 1600 trouvère and troubadour melodies to Haydn's 104 symphonies, but there are also thousands and thousands of works of folk music and popular songs. No one, even the most avid listener to music, could in an entire lifetime hear each work even once. And the amount of music increases each day.

One of the things students should learn in music classes is where a particular piece of music fits into the world of music. In the case of "Simple Gifts," the singers should acquire some understanding of the text, melodic characteristics, social setting, and similar information about this work, as well as other types of American folk music. It is not enough just to sing a song; the singers should also know something about it as a piece of music.

A difficult problem for teachers is the selection of music. With the time available for music instruction in schools so limited, teachers can barely skim the surface of the deep waters of available music. Therefore, some hard decisions must be made, and many fine works of music simply have to be left out.

Intellectual Understandings

The intellectual understandings of music involve the formation of concepts about music, the manner of thinking about music, and some knowledge of the process of creating music. Of the three, concept formation is probably the most important.

Concepts. The dictionary definition of *concept* is useful in understanding what concepts are and how they are formed: "the resultant of a generalizing mental operation: a generic mental image abstracted from percepts." Concepts, then, are generalizations about phenomena.

Some concepts such as music are broad in scope, while others such as tempo are more specific. The structuring of concepts of differing comprehensiveness is somewhat like the system of classification used in biology—phylum, genus, species, and so on. In music there are conceptual ideas about melody, harmony, form, rhythm, and so forth. Subconcepts of melody include ideas about contour, motive, theme, expression, and so on. And each of these subconcepts can be divided further into more specific categories.

A concept is not the same as its verbal symbol or definition; in fact, a concept can exist without a verbal symbol. A definition is merely the assignment of a verbal "handle" to something already formed in the mind. It is more accurate, for example, to think of the generalized quality of "dogness" as the concept rather than the more specific word *dog*.

People form concepts as they notice similarities and differences among objects and in the process organize and classify them. For example, they form a concept of dogness as animals with four legs and one tail, with an ability to bark and an acute sense of smell, but unable to climb trees or see in the dark, and with all the other features that make up the quality of dogness. Without previous experience with animals, definitions ("A dog is . . .") and factual statements ("Dogs can bark . . .") are largely meaningless. A concept must first exist on which to affix the verbal symbol. What this means is that teachers are limited to establishing situations in which the students can form the desired concepts. The generalizing process essential for concept formation must happen within each student's mind. Like the sense of musical syntax, concepts are refined somewhat with each experience. They are never learned once and for all.

The reason that teachers should be interested in concept formation is that concepts facilitate the ability to think. The fact that words are mental tools as well as a means of communication was established many years ago (Oléron, 1977). Students who have no concept of melody are seriously impaired in their ability to think about, understand, and appreciate melodies. Furthermore, because concepts are generalized ideas, they are far more versatile and flexible than specific ideas. The concept of melody can be applied in all kinds of pieces of music, but the melody to "Simple Gifts" is specific to only that one piece of music. A third virtue of conceptual learning is that basic, general ideas are remembered much better and longer than specific facts.

Way of Thinking.   Every field of study—science, history, music—has its mode of thinking, its way of looking at things. A physicist, for example, is interested in the physical properties of sounds; a social scientist is interested in the effect of sounds on human behavior; a musician is interested in how sounds are manipulated and the tonal effects and compositions that can be created with them. Part of what students should learn in school is to think somewhat as scientists in a science class, as social scientists in a social science class, and as musicians in a music class. The appropriate manner of thinking and mental approach is as much a part of the subject as is the factual information associated with it.

And how does musicianlike thinking differ from other thinking? If you question the proverbial "man on the street" about his views on music, the chances are that you will find that he thinks of music as something for accompanying other activities such as whistling songs while painting a fence and playing music on the car radio while driving to work. Almost never will he talk about music as an object for careful consideration by itself. On the other hand, musicians value organized sounds; they think that the way Mozart put sounds together in the last movement of his Symphony No. 41 is pretty impressive. In fact, they don't want distractions like painting a fence while listening to the *Jupiter* Symphony. Also, musicians analyze the sounds they listen to; they are interested in figuring out what Mozart did with the sounds. Because they value sounds and analyze them, musicians enjoy music more and know more about it than do nonmusicians.

Creative Process.   Learning in music should not be confined to the re-creation of what others have done. At a level consistent with their musical development, students should engage in creating music through composition and/or improvisation. Creative activity is valuable because it requires students to think about how sounds are manipulated, which is a central feature of the way musicians think. It also educates students about the process of creating music, including its mental trial and error and just plain hard work. In addition, creative activities allow students to explore their own music potential and in that sense to know themselves better.

As valuable as creative activities are for students in learning music, they are only a part of the subject. Students should not be confined to only those works that they themselves create, any more than they should be limited to works that someone else has created.

Skills and Activities

The words *skills* and *activities* are not synonymous. Skills refer to physical activities such as vibrato on the violin, tonguing on the clarinet, and sight-singing. Some music classes have the acquisition of skills as a major part of their content. This fact is true of the instrumental music classes and of private instruction in singing or on an instrument. Other music classes include some learning of skills.

Activities are actions that the students engage in as a means of learning. Other things being equal, students who sing a song are more likely to understand and appreciate the song than are students who just listen to it, especially if the students have not had much musical experience. For example, when English teachers want their students to understand drama, they have them read a play and discuss its purpose, literature, and technical production. To increase their understanding of certain points, English teachers may have the students act out a portion of a play in the classroom. The activity furthers their learning about drama, just as activities in music can aid learning in music.

Activities, however, cannot substitute for subject matter content. Singing one song after another, class after class, does not contribute much to the students' understanding of music or their aesthetic sensitivity. This was the flaw in Vito Amata's teaching described earlier in this chapter. At one time, music programs in the elementary schools were described entirely in terms of activities: singing, playing instruments, rhythmic movement, reading, creating, and listening. Although it may seem like hairsplitting, these were activities, not subject matter content. It would have been more accurate to say what students learned through the activity of singing or listening. The goal of music education is not just to do something in music. Rather, it is to educate students in music, and it happens that this education is often furthered through the use of appropriate activities.

The division of the subject matter content of music into activities and outcomes, or any other system of categorizing the topic, is, of course, somewhat artificial. A musical experience is a complex, unitary experience in which most of the categories are involved at the same time. When students sing or play pieces of music, they are usually strengthening their concept about music, gaining some information about it, improving their skill at performing it, and affecting how they feel about the piece in particular and music in general. The extent to which each of these results is achieved depends partly on what the teacher chooses to emphasize. Sometimes music teachers concentrate so much on one category of outcomes that little is accomplished in other categories. Effective music instruction avoids this pitfall. It strikes a reasonable balance among the making, understanding, and valuing of music, regardless of the level or type of class.

Figure 6.1 is a representation of the various aspects of content in music. The horizontal lines through the middle of the figure mark the distinction between

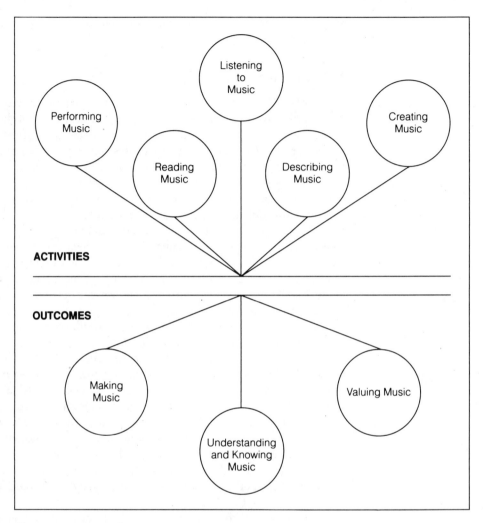

Figure 6.1   *The various aspects of content in music.*

activities and outcomes. The activities of performing, listening, creating, reading, and describing or analyzing are related through connecting lines to each other and to making, understanding and knowing, and valuing music.

Attitudes

How a person feels about what he or she knows is important. This statement is probably truer for music than for the traditional academic subjects. All of us use the ability to read and write daily, regardless of whether or not we enjoyed reading or writing when we were taught them in school. Nearly everyone needs to balance checkbooks and compute income taxes regardless of how he or she felt about arithmetic in school. Not so with music. People who don't like music can refrain from buying recordings and attending concerts. If forced to listen to music in the supermarket, they can psychologically "tune it out." Much of the ultimate success of music instruction depends on how the students feel about the subject after the classes are over. And students do acquire attitudes about the subject whether or not teachers realize it. The question is not "Will the students form feelings about music?" but rather "What feelings will they develop?"

Attitudes and knowledge are complementary. People cannot have intelligent reactions to something they don't know. If asked, "Do you like aardvarks?" they will probably answer, "I don't know." So a teacher's first task is to remove ignorance so that at the least there can be intelligent preferences and at the best there can be what educator-philosopher Harry Broudy refers to as "enlightened cherishing" (1968, p. 13). Few people, including music teachers, enjoy all types of music equally well. Being educated about something does not mean that you must like it. Rather, education offers the opportunity to make intelligent choices.

What influences the attitudes people adopt? Some generalizations can be offered in terms of tendencies, but no rules can be stated that people invariably follow. One generalization concerns familiarity. If there be truth in the statement "I know what I like," there is also truth in the words "I like what I know." Social scientists have discovered this fact in a variety of situations ranging from people to words to pictures (Kurst-Wilson & Zajonc, 1980).

People tend to like things that are similar to what they already know and like. A person who likes Broadway musicals can more easily acquire a favorable attitude toward art music than can a rock-ribbed lover of country music.

People are influenced by the person who is suggesting a change. A teacher who is liked is more effective in changing attitudes than one who isn't. Part of the reason for this tendency lies in the fact that the students have a pleasant association with the subject when they like the teacher. And the associations people make with music can influence their attitude toward it.

Attitudes are also influenced by what one's friends and peers think, and this is especially true of students in the secondary schools. If all your friends like a particular piece of music, the chances are greatly increased that you will like it, too. This is so partly because you respect and like your friends, partly because you don't want the friction involved in disagreeing with them, and partly because you tend to "go with the flow" of their feelings as you perceive them.

The family has a significant influence on children's attitudes. If the parents listen to symphonies on their record-playing equipment or tapes, the chances are much greater that the children will end up listening to that type of music when they are mature.

Guidelines for Selecting Content

Because time is limited for music instruction, teachers must make some difficult decisions about what to teach. In doing so, they may consult students and parents and consider their wishes. Even when this is done, however, teachers have to make choices. The following guidelines may help in doing this.

Educational. The first guideline sounds like a simple one: The students should gain information, skills, or attitudes that they did not have prior to the class or course and probably would not acquire without instruction in school. This idea seems basic to any educational undertaking. Without it, education becomes merely baby-sitting or a recreation program.

While the guideline is a simple but important one, it has sometimes not been followed, for a number of reasons. Some teachers have felt that the effort to teach something would not be worth it, or that it would not make any difference to the students, or that there is not really anything to learn in music. Whatever the reason, the students were the losers.

One practical question for the criterion of being educational is, "What would the students learn about music if they had no instruction in school?" Is there some music and information about music that, like riding a bicycle, would probably be learned without a music teacher? The music that can be learned outside of school can be left to others and other subject matter content can be taught in the schools.

Valid. Music is an established academic discipline, a recognized field of knowledge and study. Teachers should ask themselves, "Is what is being taught a legitimate portion of the field of music? Would most trained musicians (performers, musicologists, teachers) recognize and accept this content as a part of the field?" For example, a few teachers of violin with elementary school children use a kind of notation in which notes are identified not by pitch but by the name of the string and fingering: A1, D3, and so on. The system cannot indicate relative pitch, note values, or sharps and flats. It must be unlearned as the students progress. No music theorist, symphony musician, or musicologist uses this system in studying or playing music. Therefore, it is not valid in the field of music.

The call for validity is a logical one. Why teach something under the name of music that is not really part of the field of music? It is neither logical nor honest to transform a subject, even in the hope of aiding learning.

Fundamental. Closely related to validity of content is the belief that students should learn the basic ideas of the subject, not just factual minutiae. Knowing the keys of the thirty-two Beethoven piano sonatas is not as useful as understanding his development of themes and motives. When information is associated with a concept, it is useful, but memorizing insignificant facts is not effective learning. Fundamental ideas—tonality, development of themes, the 2:1 ratio in rhythmic notation, and the unity of words and music in art songs, to cite a few examples— are valuable because they are comprehensive and have wide application in music.

Representative. If the music curriculum is limited to only a few types or aspects of music, then the students are not being given a well-balanced education in music. The band director who has the band play one march after another and the general music teacher who spends all the class time working with the synthesizer are both guilty of shortchanging their students, because both are omitting many other important areas of music. Sometimes teachers give the students very little art music—

music that contains a sophisticated handling of sounds. Their students continue to think of music only as a pastime or entertainment and are never introduced to the idea that music is an aesthetic, expressive human creation.

One way of checking out the representativeness of music selected is to take a piece of paper or a chalkboard and divide it into boxes according to categories. On the horizontal plane one might put style periods: pre-Renaissance, Renaissance, Baroque, Classical, Romantic, and Twentieth Century. On the vertical plane could be put types of music appropriate for the class, such as folk songs, show tunes, art songs, opera-oratorio, and religious works for a choral group. Making a mark in the appropriate category for each piece of music provides a good picture of the distribution of the music used.

Contemporary. The music and information taught in music classes should be up to date. This criterion refers not only to the date when composed but also to the style. Some works composed in the 1960s and 1970s are still in a style that is a century old. The main problem for teachers in this matter is the technical difficulty of many twentieth-century works. They would like to have the students sing or play them, but many times the music is too hard. It requires some searching, but contemporary works that are not technically so demanding can be found.

Relevant. The word *relevant* has been used in several ways in recent years. To some people it means those things vital for survival and living; to others it means topics that one happens to like or be interested in; and to others it means the relationship between a person and a given subject. It is in the third sense that the word is used here.

Sometimes the interests of the students and the requirements of valid subject matter have appeared to be in conflict. Proponents of subject matter validity ask, "What good is a subject that has lost its integrity and character?" The advocates of relevance answer, "What good is a subject that seems meaningless and worthless to the students?" Both views have a fair claim for the attention of teachers, and the two positions need not be mutually exclusive.

Relevance is probably affected more by the method of teaching than by the content. Topics and subjects have little inherent relevance; people make things relevant. A topic that is important and interesting to one person couldn't matter less to another. Relevance results when a topic is given meaning through a teacher's attitude and skill in organizing the subject. Teachers need to teach so that the real content of music becomes relevant to the students. For example, figuring out minor scale patterns is not relevant to most students because it is not particularly helpful to them in understanding music. Achieving relevance is quite an assignment, but the job of teaching music well is not an easy one.

Learnable. The music curriculum must be learnable by most of the students. It is useless to teach something for which they are not prepared. While the students' backgrounds and interests should be considered, these are not the only factors that teachers should think about. Teaching a piece of music that is of a suitable level of difficulty for the students should be determined in relation to the other guidelines, as well as to a host of practical matters such as amount of class time, books and materials, and performance obligations. A good teacher can build on the interests the students already have without abandoning the subject. If students seem un-interested in a worthy topic, perhaps another approach to it is called for instead of giving up on it entirely.

Some of the guidelines presented here may appear to be contradictory, and to a degree this is so. The need to offer substantive instruction seems to work against the idea of relevancy, and contemporary content appears to contradict the idea of representative samples of the subject. In the case of education versus relevancy, the solution lies in the proper methods of teaching. However, some of the time teachers need to strike a balance in making curricular decisions between conflict-ing needs. None of the guidelines are absolute and overriding, which means that teachers have to account for a number of divergent factors in their teaching. A clear understanding of the subject matter content is essential for good teaching. For this reason, future music teachers need to teach concepts and skills from a carefully selected menu of music and music-related activities.

Questions

1. What five things could students in band be learning when they play "Stars and Stripes Forever" by Sousa?

2. Give examples of three different types of musical skills.

3. Why is a sense of musical syntax important in learning music?

4. What is a concept?

5. Why should students form concepts about music?

6. How would musicianlike thinking about the song "Simple Gifts" differ from everyday, ordinary thinking about it?

7. Why should students in nonperforming music classes engage in some musical activities such as singing or playing simple instruments?

8. What is the difference between an outcome and an activity?

9. Why is it very desirable for students in music classes to acquire favorable attitudes toward the subject?

10. What factors affect the attitudes people adopt?

11. What does the word *valid* mean in discussions of curriculum?

12. What does the word *relevant* mean in discussions of curriculum?

Projects

1. Make a list of the music skills and knowledge that most students will learn without the benefit of instruction in music. Then, make a list of music skills and knowledge for which most students need instruction if they are to learn them to any reasonable extent.

2. Select a piece of music for use with a class or performing group. List what the students could learn from studying it.

3. For the musical work you selected for the project, describe why it is or could be
   a. valid,
   b. fundamental, and
   c. relevant.

References Broudy, H. S. (1968). The case for aesthetic education. In R. A. Choate (Ed.), *Documentary report of the Tanglewood Symposium* (p. 13). Reston, VA: Music Educators National Conference.

Kurst-Wilson, W. R., & Zajonc, R. B. (1980). Affective discrimination of stimuli that cannot be recognized. *Science, 207*, 557–558.

Oléron, P. (1977). *Language and mental development.* (R. P. Lorion, Trans.). Hillsdale, NJ: Lawrence Erlbaum.

Penfield, W., & Roberts, T. (1959). *Speech and brain—mechanisms.* Princeton, NJ: Princeton University Press.

CHAPTER 7

The Development of the Profession

*B*ecause music has been around since the dawn of civilization, the teaching of music, at least in an informal way, has also been around a long time. The first major writings on the value of learning music come from the ancient Greeks around 400 B.C. Plato believed strongly in the doctrine of *ethos*—the idea that music affected moral character. For this reason, he advocated music in the education of every citizen, which in those days was a rather exclusive status. Some movement instruction involving rhythm was included in physical education, but we would probably not recognize what was taught as being music in today's terms.

In the Middle Ages, music was considered one of the seven liberal arts along with grammar, logic, rhetoric, arithmetic, astronomy, and geometry. It was, therefore, included in the curriculum of the universities that were being founded in Italy, France, and England. The fascination with music was not with its artistic or tonal properties but rather with its acoustical ratios and other mathematical properties. These were thought to hold certain secrets of the cosmos. The study of music consisted of thinking and talking about music, not performing it.

A more practical type of music education was found in the conservatories, which were founded in the 1500s. The word *conservatory* comes from the Italian word for orphanage, and, indeed, early conservatories were also orphanages. One can only guess why orphans were selected to be trained as performers. Perhaps it

was believed that because they had no families, a life "on the road" (typical of musicians in those days) would not bother them.

Music was undoubtedly taught on an individual, one-to-one basis, especially to women of the upper classes and to boys who were going to make their livelihoods as musicians. But music education in the schools and colleges as we know it today is a relatively recent development.

MUSIC EDUCATION IN AMERICA

Before 1800

European music came to America with the first settlers to Virginia and Massachusetts, but it is not clear when professional instruction in music began. The first music instruction books were the product of John Tufts, a minister, who in the early eighteenth century wanted to teach the churchgoing colonists to sing psalms and hymns. He devised a tetrachord system of notation in which the octave is broken into two identical halves. Tufts chose the tetrachords E F G A and B C D E, which he identified by the syllables *mi, fa, sol,* and *la* (Lowens, 1964). His system was later adapted into "shape notes" in which each of the four shapes of the note heads indicates a syllable. Shape notes are still seen occasionally in the notation of some hymnals, especially in the southern states.

Tufts' efforts were followed by the "singing school" movement in which music teachers traveled from one town to another to give lessons for a few weeks. The singing schools existed primarily to teach church music.

The Nineteenth Century

A Swiss educator by the name of Johann Heinrich Pestalozzi had a major influence on education in the first half of the nineteenth century. Although he was not a music teacher himself, his ideas were adapted by others for the teaching of music. One adaptation was by George Nageli, who wrote a book in 1810 entitled *The Theory of Instruction in Singing According to Pestalozzian Principles* (*Die Gesangbildumstehre nach Pestalozzischen Grundsatzen*). Another early proponent of Pestalozzian ideas was Joseph H. Naef, who had been a member of Pestalozzi's staff in Europe before emigrating to America in 1806. In 1809, he founded an elementary school, and in 1830, he presented his ideas on music teaching according the principles of Pestalozzi.

1. To teach sounds before signs—to make the child learn to sing before he learns the written notes or their names;
2. To lead him to observe by hearing and imitating sounds, their resemblances and differences, their agreeable and disagreeable effects, instead of explaining these things to him—in short, to make active instead of passive in learning;
3. To teach but one thing at a time—rhythm, melody, and expression are to be taught and practiced separately, before the child is called to the difficult task of attending to all at once;
4. In making them practice each step of these divisions, until they are master of it, before passing to the next;
5. In giving the principles and theory after the practice, and as induction from it;
6. To analyze and practice the elements of articulate sound in order to apply them to music;
7. To have the names of the notes correspond to those used in instrumental music. (Birge, 1966, pp. 38–39)

Lowell Mason is generally considered to be the father of music in American schools. He was a man of enormous vitality, versatility, and vision who became convinced that instruction in music was good for all children. In 1836, he petitioned the school board in Boston for the inclusion of vocal music in the elementary schools. A special committee of the board was appointed to consider the proposal. In 1837, it submitted a report containing a positive recommendation. The report is interesting not only for its quaint syntax but also for the reasons it provides to justify the introduction of music in the Boston schools:

Let music be examined by the following standards:—
1. Intellectually. Music had its place among the seven liberal arts, which scholastic ages regarded as pertaining to humanity. Arithmetic, Geometry, Astronomy, and Music—these formed the quadrivium. Memory, comparison, attention, intellectual faculties—all of them are quickened by a study of its principles. It may be made to some extent a mental discipline.

2. Morally. It is unphilosophical to say that exercises in vocal music may not be so directed and arranged as to produce those habits of feeling of which these sounds are the type. Happiness, contentment, cheerfulness, tranquillity—these are the natural effects of music.
3. Physically. It appears self evident that exercises in vocal music, when not carried to an unreasonable excess, must expand the chest and thereby strengthen the lungs and vital organs. Judging then by this triple standard, intellectually, morally, and physically, vocal music seems to have a natural place in every system of instruction which aspires, as should every system, to develop man's whole nature. (Birge, 1966, p. 41)

Later it continues:

What is the great object of our system of popular instruction? Are our schools mere houses of correction, in which animal nature is to be kept in subjection by the law of brute force and the stated drudgery of distasteful tasks? Not so. They have a nobler office. They are valuable mainly as a preparation and a training of the young spirit for usefulness and happiness in coming life. Now, the defect of our present system, admirable as that system is, is this, that it aims to develop the intellectual part of man's nature solely when, for all the true purposes of life, it is of more importance, a hundredfold, to feel rightly than to think profoundly. Besides, human life must and ought to have its amusements. Through vocal music you set in motion a mighty power which silently, but surely, in the end, will humanize, refine and elevate a whole community.

From this place first went out the great principle, that the property of all should be taxed for the education of all. From this place, also, may the example, in this country, first go forth of that education rendered more complete by the introduction by public authority, of vocal music into our system of popular instruction. (Birge, 1966, p. 47)

The Twentieth Century

It is difficult for us who live in the final years of the twentieth century to imagine what life and education were like in 1900. Americans lived mainly on farms and in small towns. The automobile and telephone were just beginning to appear; radio was a couple decades in the future, and television was still four decades away. A woman's place was generally understood to be in the home, and most men were employed at jobs that required physical labor—farming, mining, and so on. Having enough food and place to live was a major concern in life, because neither could be assumed. There was no social security system or unemployment or medical insurance. Life expectancy was much shorter.

Education was different, too. Most young people did not attend school beyond sixth or eighth grade. They went to small, one-room schools in which rote learning prevailed. Most teachers were single women (getting married meant giving up their teaching jobs), and they had less than a year of training beyond high school at a teaching training institution. Few teenagers went to high school, which offered mainly a college preparatory program laden with subjects such as Latin, algebra, history, and the like. There were no football games or other extracurricular activities or subjects such as home economics and typing. Music education was almost entirely vocal music. In many schools it consisted of a little singing by rote, while in other schools it included much drill on sight-singing.

Changes of enormous importance were on the horizon in 1900, however. Not only would America begin to grow in size and importance in the world, it would also change from a rural to an urban nation. Society was to become far more complex, and the roles of women and minorities were to change greatly. Schools were changing, too. For example, from 10 percent of the potential number of students attending high school in 1900, the percentage increased to over 70 percent by 1940 (Department of Health, Education, and Welfare, 1970). Along with this change came a much richer and more varied curriculum, one that included both instrumental and choral music. Surprising as it may seem today, the first instrumental groups in the schools were orchestras, not bands. In places like Richmond, Indiana, and Winfield, Kansas, enterprising teachers such as Will Earhart and Edgar B. Gordon were developing effective instrumental music programs.

After World War I. Following their service in the war, a number of military band directors began teaching in the schools, which led to an interest in bands. Several group instrumental methods were published, and high-quality music programs were beginning in major cities such as Cleveland, Los Angeles, Chicago, Detroit, Cincinnati, Kansas City, and others.

The growth of music, especially instrumental music, was so rapid in the 1920s and 1930s that people trained to teach at the high school level were in short supply. As further discussed in Chapter 8, this had a profound effect on the type of instruction offered. This movement of professional musicians into teaching was accelerated by the introduction of "talking pictures" in 1927 (with its loss of pit orchestra jobs in theaters) and by the Great Depression that began in 1929 (with its general unemployment).

These years also saw the beginning of the progressive education movement. Based on the ideas of philosopher-educator John Dewey, the movement emphasized the learning process rather than subject matter content and the need for a correlation between the students' school and life experiences. Two results of such thinking were an emphasis on the involvement of the classroom teacher in the teaching of music and the correlation of music with other school subjects, especially social studies.

At the same time, however, conflict existed in music education over the importance of sight-singing. A sizable number of music educators advocated much drill and practice in reading music so that students would gain enough skill in reading music to participate in music throughout the rest of their lives. Other music educators saw music largely as an enrichment of the children's lives and somewhat of a handmaiden to other subject matter areas. As with so many disputes, this one was never completely resolved.

After World War II. The 1940s were consumed first with the conduct of the war and then later with the recovery from that conflict. The decades of the 1950s and 1960s were good ones for education in a number of ways. The number of children in school represented a high-water mark in terms of the percentage of the population, reaching a level that may never be equaled again. This situation meant that there were a lot of families who were very supportive of the schools. In addition, there was a faith in education as a means of improving society and life. Music programs enjoyed unprecedented growth during these decades.

The 1960s. This decade is especially interesting because of the number and size of the nationwide programs that appeared. To begin with, a wave of concern over the quality of the schools filled newspapers and popular magazines. Much of the same language heard in the cries for school reform in the 1960s would be similar to that heard again in the 1980s. In the 1960s, the responses to the calls for reform were a number of major grants from the federal government for a wide variety of projects. In other cases, professional organizations, including MENC, also sponsored large national events and projects.

Probably the best known of these national events for music educators was the Tanglewood Symposium, which was held at Tanglewood in Massachusetts for two weeks during the summer of 1967. Its theme was "Music in a Democratic Society," and its participants included leaders from business, education, labor, government, and the arts, as well as music educators. The many papers read and the conclusions to the discussion held during the symposium were published in a documentary report. The final declaration of the symposium stated the following:

> Music Educators at Tanglewood agree that:
> 1. Music serves best when its integrity as an art is maintained.
> 2. Music of all periods, styles, forms, and cultures belongs in the curriculum. The musical repertory should be expanded to involve music of our time in its rich variety, including currently popular teenage music and avant-garde music, American folk music, and the music of other cultures.
> 3. Schools and colleges should provide adequate time for music programs ranging from preschool through adult or continuing education.
> 4. Instruction in the arts should be a general and important part of education in the senior high school.
> 5. Developments in educational technology, educational television, programmed instruction, and computer-assisted instruction should be applied to music study and research.
> 6. Greater emphasis should be placed on helping the individual student to fulfill his needs, goals, and potentials.
> 7. The music education profession must contribute its skills, proficiencies and insights toward assisting in the solution of urgent social problems as in the "inner city" or other areas with culturally deprived individuals.
> 8. Programs of teacher education must be expanded and improved to provide music teachers who are specially equipped to teach high school courses in the history and literature of music, courses in the humanities and related arts, as well as teachers equipped to work with the very young, with adults, with the disadvantaged, and with the emotionally disturbed. (Choate, 1968, p. 139)

The effects of the symposium were felt in music education long after the event itself was over. It provided direction for a number of MENC efforts, as well as topics for special issues of the *Music Educators Journal*.

Another event that garnered much publicity was the Yale Seminar held at Yale University in 1963. Unlike the Tanglewood Symposium, which was developed by

MENC and supported by the Presser Foundation, the Yale Seminar was the result of a grant from the U.S. Office of Education, forerunner to the present-day Department of Education. The seminar, which included only a few music educators, was quite critical of a number of aspects of music education. The main criticism concerned the quality of the music used in the schools, both as to its artistic worth and its coverage in terms of ethnic and popular types of music.

An outgrowth of the Yale Seminar was the Juilliard Repertory Project, which was a major funding effort of the U.S. Office of Education. Begun in 1964, it was supported by a large grant from the U.S. Office of Education to the Juilliard School of Music to develop a body of authentic and meaningful music to enrich the repertoire of music available to music teachers in the elementary schools. The music was compiled by three groups: musicologists, music education leaders, and school music teachers. The music was divided into seven categories, based on historical style periods, plus folk music. The selection process was for the musicologists to select material and then submit the works to a panel of leaders in music education, who decided which works would be field-tested in the schools.

Four hundred pieces of music were tested, with 230 vocal and instrumental works being retained for the Juilliard Repertory Library. This collection was published by Canyon Press of Cincinnati. Because of the amount of material (384 pages), the collection is also published in eight volumes of vocal music and four of instrumental music.

Two projects of the 1960s promoted creativity and new music. The most important of these was the Young Composers Project, which began in 1957 with a grant from the Ford Foundation. The idea was to place ten young (under thirty-five) composers as composers-in-residence in school systems with strong music programs. The hope was that the young composer would learn about the opportunities and challenges of writing for school groups and that in return the school and community would benefit and its interest in contemporary music would be increased. The first year of operation for the project was 1959, and by 1962 thirty-one composers had been placed in school systems. In many ways the response to the program was good, but the composers reported that many music teachers were poorly prepared to deal with contemporary idioms. Therefore, in 1962 the project was increased to become one of the Ford Foundation's ten major programs. MENC submitted a proposal to the foundation for what was to become the Contemporary Music Project (CMP), and the idea was funded in the amount of $1,380,000. The purposes of the project were as follows:

1. To increase the emphasis on the creative aspect of music in the public schools;
2. To create a solid foundation or environment in the music education profession for the acceptance, through understanding, of the contemporary music idiom;
3. To reduce the compartmentalization that now exists between the profession of music composition and music education for the benefit of composers and music educators alike;

4. To cultivate taste and discrimination on the part of music educators and students regarding the quality of contemporary music used in schools; and

5. To discover, when possible, creative talent among students. ("Contemporary Music Project," 1973, p. 34)

The practice of placing composers in the schools continued, but the CMP added to that effort by establishing workshops and seminars at various colleges throughout the United States to educate teachers about contemporary music through analyzing, performing, and creating music. Six pilot projects were also established in the schools. Following the Northwestern University seminar in 1965, six regional institutes for Music in Contemporary Education, involving thirty-six educational institutions, were formed. In 1968 the Ford Foundation gave another $1,340,000 to MENC, which contributed $250,000, for a five-year extension of the program. Some modest changes were made in the composer project, and twenty-one teachers were given grants to write curriculum materials using the methods and music from the CMP. The CMP ended in 1973.

During its final ten years, the CMP devoted much of its attention to the skills and knowledge required to deal with all types of music. Its approach was a process-centered one that included three components: performing, organizing, and describing. This manner of teaching was often referred to as the "common elements approach." Through this approach, the CMP maintained, the compartmentalization in the music profession could be greatly reduced. No longer, for example, would the trumpet or voice teacher in the studio be concerned only with the performance of a musical work, but would also point out its theoretical and historical aspects.

Although it may not have met all its goals, the CMP clearly had an impact on the music education profession. Many music teachers are now more conscious of the need to teach and use some twentieth-century music. The elementary school music series books described in the next chapter now contain a good representation of the various types of contemporary music, and publishers have brought out more contemporary materials for use by school groups.

Not only has there been more interest in recent years in creative efforts in music classes, the form these efforts have taken has been broadened. When the topic was mentioned in the elementary music series books and methods books forty years ago, it was usually a description of how a class could compose a song together. Today individual efforts in creating music are emphasized, and they include sound pieces, works of electronic music, ostinato accompaniments, improvising phrases, and short songs. The music series books offer suggestions for creating music with tape-recorded sounds or with sounds located around the classroom and for creating or improvising simple parts on classroom instruments. Theory classes at the high school level also often contain a number of creative activities.

An effort that promoted creativity was the Manhattanville Music Curriculum Project (MMCP). The program was funded by grants from the U.S. Office of Education and was named for Manhattanville College of the Sacred Heart in Purchase,

New York, where it began in 1965. At first it was an exploratory program to locate and identify innovative and experimental music programs throughout the United States. Ninety-two programs were studied, fifteen of them in depth. The portion of the MMCP for which it is best known today began in 1966 and consisted of three phases spread over three years. The first phase studied how students learn, curriculum, and classroom procedures. The second phase was a refinement and synthesis of the information gained in the first phase in a course of study. The third phase consisted of field testing and refinements, as well as plans for teacher training and assessment. The project ended before the assessment could be conducted.

The MMCP program attempted to have children learn to hear music the way a composer does—that is, to perceive music without having first to interpret it cognitively. The children were to think in the medium of music and to study music as a whole to experience all aspects of music. Students were asked to compose, perform, conduct, listen, and not to stand back and consider music reverently (Thomas, 1968). A music lab was advocated as the needed physical setup for achieving these goals, and individual or small group activities were the means. Learning in the MMCP view is essentially problem solving; each problem solved leads to a new synthesis and increasing insight into music.

The field tests of the program in phase three revealed that some modifications were called for and that teacher in-service training was needed. The MMCP personnel had four concerns about the music teachers who were involved in the field trials:

1. Teachers did not know enough about music to work with students creatively.
2. Teachers found it difficult to consider goals other than skill achievement and performance.
3. Many teachers were method-oriented and found it difficult to work in a new framework.
4. Many teachers had not personally experienced creative accomplishment and were therefore not secure in an atmosphere of creativity. (Mark, 1986, p. 137)

The teacher reeducation program devised by the MMCP required from sixty to ninety hours of instruction.

For some of the reasons cited, many music teachers have found the MMCP program difficult to establish in their schools. In addition, its requirement of a music lab and a sizable amount of teacher time also greatly inhibited its adoption. And the fact that the MMCP consisted almost entirely of creative activity may have caused most music teachers to reject it.

The 1960s were a time of much activity in arts and education on the part of the federal government. These efforts took the form of two major pieces of legislation: the Elementary and Secondary Education Act of 1965 and the National Foundation on the Arts and Humanities. The Elementary and Secondary Education Act provided massive funding ($1.3 billion in 1965) in five sections called "titles." Title I provided grants to schools for the education of disadvantaged children. The nature of the services supported with these funds was left up to the local school, and music instruction or activity could be included under this title. Title II provided for the purchase of library resources and instructional materials. Titles III and IV supported local and regional research and development centers. Title V sought to strengthen state departments of education. Because the largest amount of money was provided under Title I, it had the most impact. Some school districts hired music teachers and purchased music books and equipment for use in areas with large numbers of low-income families. It was estimated that about one-third of the 8.3 million children receiving the benefits of Title I were involved with music or art (Lehman, 1968).

Legislation establishing the National Foundations on the Arts and the Humanities was also enacted in 1965 "to help create and sustain not only a climate encouraging freedom of thought, imagination, and inquiry, but also the material conditions facilitating the release of this creative talent" (National Endowment for the Arts [NEA], 1975, p. 3). The National Endowment for the Arts and the National Endowment for the Humanities are both agencies under this legislative action. During the first years of the NEA, its education efforts consisted mainly of its Artists-in-Schools program in which professional performers and artists provided performances or special instruction on a visiting basis. In recent years the NEA has attempted to assume a more significant role in curriculum and other educational matters. The NEA's effectiveness has been limited by the small amount of funds (at least in terms of federal programs) and its promotion of programs to give artists and musicians employment. The educational impact of such programs appears to have been a secondary consideration.

Everything considered, however, the 1960s were a good time for education and the arts. Not only was there much innovative activity, there was also much growth and improvement.

The 1970s. The decade started out well for education, but some long-term trends were soon to have their negative impact. For one, the national programs of the 1960 failed to have anywhere near the impact their supporters had hoped for. Many of the curriculum projects developed materials that were too difficult or did not relate well to the students and teachers for whom they were intended. The result was a disenchantment with such efforts. Then, the percentage of the population with children in school was decreasing following the "baby boom" of the 1950s and 1960s, while the number of teachers exceeded demand. The result was the "riffing" (reduction in force) of many teachers and the hiring of few beginning teachers. In addition, the competition for tax dollars became more intense with demands for health care, benefits for the elderly, law enforcement and prisons, and so on. As taxes seemed to follow an inevitable upward path, taxpayers dug in their heels by approving Proposition 13 in California and Proposition 2½ in Massachusetts. Both of these propositions placed severe restrictions on the funds raised from property taxes, which traditionally had been a major source of revenue for schools.

The decade was not without some attention to education at the national level. The Education for All Handicapped Children Act was enacted in 1975. This legislation mandated special education for handicapped students. Although some states had been providing programs for these students, it was estimated that before this legislation, only half of the 8 million handicapped children were receiving any kind of arts education (Graham, 1975).

The law had two effects for music teachers. One was to require some of them to become competent in teaching music to children with special needs—the emotionally disturbed, the physically handicapped, the mentally retarded, and so on. The second result was the mainstreaming of handicapped students into music classes. The regulations for the law require that "to the maximum extent appropriate, handicapped children . . . are educated with children who are not handicapped . . ." and that "special classes, separate schooling or other removal of handicapped children from the regular educational environment occurs only when the nature or severity of the handicap is such that education in regular classes with the use of supplementary aids and services cannot be achieved satisfactorily" (*Federal Register,* 1977, p. 42497). MENC has long maintained that music teachers should be involved in placement decisions for handicapped students in music classes (MENC, 1986). This suggestion often has been ignored by school principals, with the result that in some cases mainstreaming has caused serious problems in the educating of the other students.

The 1980s. A combination of circumstances led to renewed national concern in the 1980s about the quality of education in American schools. One was America's decreasing ability to compete economically with Japan and Germany—two of the countries it had defeated in World War II thirty-five years earlier. There was a clear need for a better-educated work force. Another circumstance was the decline of scores received by high school juniors and seniors on the Scholastic Aptitude Test (SAT). Although the SAT tests only the ability to do academic work, not achievement, and despite the fact that many more students were taking such tests (which meant that the test population was less selected than in the past), these scores were seen by many persons in the media and politics as evidence of a general decline in the quality of the education of American students. Another concern was the deterioration of the school systems in so many major cities. Crime, drugs, and absenteeism seemed to have replaced learning.

The response in the 1980s to perceived educational problems was not in large-scale federally funded programs, as was true in the 1960s. Instead, it was in highly publicized reports (which required only a tiny expenditure of funds compared to new educational programs), some sponsored by the federal government and others by private foundations. The best known of these reports was a product of the National Commission on Excellence in Education. The commission, appointed by President Reagan and made up of businessmen and educators, issued a report in 1983 entitled *A Nation at Risk: The Imperative for Educational Reform.* Its ringing phrases claimed many weaknesses in American education—diluted curricula, limited class time, not very able teachers, and insufficient requirements, and a general lack of academic rigor. The report suggested the following, more demanding graduation requirements: four years of English, three years of mathematics, three years of science, three years of social studies, and one-half year of computer science. College-bound students were urged also to take two years of a foreign language.

Unfortunately, *A Nation at Risk* mentions the arts only twice. At one point it urges "rigorous efforts in subjects that advance students' personal, educational, and occupational goals, such as the fine and performing arts and vocational education" (National Commission on Excellence in Education, 1983, p. 26). (Note the combining of the arts with vocational education.) The other reference to the arts concerns the eight grades of schooling before high school. The report states that they "should be specifically designed to provide a sound base for study in those and later years in such areas as English language development and writing, computation and problem-solving skills, science, social studies, foreign language, and the arts" (National Commission on Excellence in Education, 1983, p. 27).

Another major report on education was the College Entrance Examination Board's publication *Academic Preparation for College: What Students Need to Know and Be Able to Do* (College Entrance Examination Board, 1983). In contrast to *A Nation at Risk,* it speaks out strongly for the arts by including them along with English, mathematics, science, social science, and foreign languages as one of the six major areas of study. Because of the high quality of the College Board's expression about the importance of the arts, a sizable portion of the work is cited here.

Why?

The arts—visual arts, theater, music, and dance—challenge and extend human experience. They provide means of expression that go beyond ordinary speaking and writing. They can express intimate thoughts and feelings. They are a unique record of diverse cultures and how these cultures have developed over time. They provide distinctive ways of understanding human beings and nature. The arts are creative modes by which all people can enrich their lives both by self-expression and response to the expressions of others.

Works of art often involve subtle meanings and complex systems of expression. Fully appreciating such works requires the careful reasoning and sustained study that lead to informed insight. Moreover, just as thorough understanding of science requires laboratory or field work, so fully understanding the arts involves first-hand work in them.

Preparation in the arts will be valuable to college entrants whatever their intended field of study. The actual practice of the arts can engage the imagination, foster flexible ways of thinking, develop disciplined effort, and build self-confidence. Appreciation of the arts is integral to the understanding of other cultures sought in the study of history, foreign language, and social sciences. Preparation in the arts will also enable college students to engage in and profit from advanced study, performance, and studio work in the arts. For some, such college-level work will lead to careers in the arts. For many others, it will permanently enhance the quality of their lives, whether they continue artistic activity as an avocation or appreciation of the arts as observers and members of audiences.

What?

Students going to college will profit from the following preparation in the arts.

- The ability to understand and appreciate the unique qualities of each of the arts.
- The ability to appreciate how people of various cultures have used the arts to express themselves.
- The ability to understand and appreciate different artistic styles and works from representative historical periods and cultures.
- Some knowledge of the social and intellectual influences affecting artistic form.
- The ability to use the skills, media, tools, and processes required to express themselves in one or more of the arts. College entrants also will profit from more intensive preparation in at least one of the four areas of the arts: visual arts, theater, music, and dance. . . .

If the preparation of college entrants is in *music,* they will need the following knowledge and skills.

- The ability to identify and describe—using the appropriate vocabulary—various musical forms from different historical periods.
- The ability to listen perceptively to music, distinguishing such elements as pitch, rhythm, timbre, and dynamics.
- The ability to read music.
- The ability to evaluate a musical work or performance.
- To know how to express themselves by playing an instrument, singing in a group or individually, or composing music. (College Entrance Examination Board, 1983, pp. 17–18)

The response to the challenges of *A Nation at Risk* and other national reports was left largely to the states. As with the federal government, rhetoric far outdistanced meaningful action at the state level. The most common response was to increase the number of courses required for high school graduation. Generally these requirements reduced the number of electives, which in turn reduced enrollments in music. Other actions including lengthening the school day and the school year, increasing teacher certification requirements, and the testing of students and teachers, although little actual *new* testing of either teachers or students was undertaken.

Throughout much of the 1980s, music education made some modest but important gains. The losses in programs and teachers in the late 1970s and early 1980s were stemmed, and some increases were achieved. The number of college students majoring in music education began gradually to increase. MENC reflected these gains and the effects of its improved programs by reaching (in 1990) the highest number of active members in its history.

Questions   1. Prior to the late 1950s, what reasons were given for including music in the schools?

2. Which reasons (in your answer to the previous question) were based on the artistic values of music?

3. What major changes occurred in high school education between 1900 and 1940?

4. What are the main points of the Tanglewood declaration?

5. What was the major accomplishment of the Juilliard Repertory Project?

6. What were the objectives of the Contemporary Music Project?

7. What was the "common elements" approach that the Contemporary Music Project promoted?

8. What two major federal programs were passed in 1965 that affected education and the arts?

9. Under what conditions do federal regulations require that handicapped students be placed in regular classes?

10. What have been the effects of the Education for All Handicapped Children Act of 1975 on music education, especially in the elementary schools?

11. In the 1980s, what actions did state and the federal government take with regard to perceived weaknesses in education?

References

Birge, E. B. (1966). *History of public school music in the United States.* Reston, VA: Music Educators National Conference.

Choate, R. A. (Ed.). (1968). *Documentary report of the Tanglewood Symposium.* Reston, VA: Music Educators National Conference.

College Entrance Examination Board. (1983). *Academic preparation for college: What students need to know and be able to do.* New York: Carnegie Foundation.

Contemporary music project in perspective. (1973). *Music Educators Journal, 59*(9), 34.

Digest of Educational Statistics. (1970). Department of Health, Education, and Welfare. Washington, DC: U.S. Government Printing Office.

Federal Register. (1977, August 23). 42(163), 42497. (121a.550). Washington, DC: U.S. Government Printing Office.

Graham, R. M. (Comp.). (1975). *Music for the exceptional child.* Reston, VA: Music Educators National Conference.

Lehman, P. R. (1968). Federal program in support of music. *Music Educators Journal, 55*(1), 53.

Lowens, I. (1964). The first American music textbook. In *Music and musicians in early America,* pp. 39–57. New York: Norton.

Mark, M. L. (1986). *Contemporary music education* (2nd ed.). New York: Schirmer Books.

National Commission on Excellence in Education. (1983). *A nation at risk: The imperative for educational reform.* Washington, DC: U.S. Department of Education.

National Endowment for the Arts. (1975). *Guide to programs.* Washington, DC: Author.

The school music program: Description and standards (2nd ed.) (1986). Reston, VA: Music Educators National Conference.

Thomas, R. B. (1968). Learning music unconventionally—Manhattanville music curriculum program. *Music Educators Journal, 54*(9), 64.

CHAPTER 8

The Nature of the Music Program

*I*t is important for prospective teachers to be informed about and interested in the entire music program—kindergarten through high school, general, choral, and instrumental. The reason for an interest in the total program is the fact that it is a single entity. At each level or in each type of class, students are learning music, and in the long run each portion of the music program affects to some degree the other parts.

GOALS OF THE MUSIC PROGRAM

The same basic goals prevail for all portions of the music education program—band, general music, and so on. And they apply also to all levels. The amount of attention devoted to certain goals differs to some extent according to the type of class, but that does not alter the fact that the entire program is (or should be) related and coordinated from one portion to another.

Various committees have from time to time developed lists of goals for music programs. Probably the most significant of these are two publications of MENC:

Music in General Education (1965) and *The School Music Program: Description and Standards,* second edition (1986). *Music in General Education* states its goals in terms of what all students should be able to do by the time they finish high school (Ernst & Gary, 1965). Furthermore, the goals are divided into three broad categories: skills, understandings, and attitudes. They are presented here in abbreviated and paraphrased form.

Skills

1. Skill in listening to music

2. Skill in singing

3. Skill in playing a simple instrument

Understandings

4. Understand the structure and form of music

5. Understand historical development of music

6. Integrate a knowledge of the fine arts

7. Understand the place of music in society

Attitudes

8. Value music as a means of self-expression

9. Continue to grow musically

10. Discriminate with respect to music

The eleven goals listed in *Music in General Education* are not specific about what level should be achieved. For example, they do not spell out how well students should be able to sing or how much they need to know about the role of music in society. Instead, the hope was to make music educators aware of these areas so that they will be covered in some form during the twelve years of elementary and secondary school.

The *Description and Standards* book contains suggestions for the types of the learning that should take place and includes quite specific standards for staff, time, equipment, and materials for meeting those standards. It lists ten outcomes, which are quite similar to those developed by the writers of *Music in General Education.*

The elementary and secondary music program should be designed to produce individuals who:

1. are able to make music, alone and with others;
2. are able to improvise;
3. are able to use the vocabulary and notation of music;
4. are able to respond to music aesthetically, intellectually, and emotionally;
5. are acquainted with a wide variety of music, including diverse musical styles and genres;
6. understand the role music has played and continues to play in the lives of human beings;
7. are able to make aesthetic judgments based on critical listening and analysis;
8. have developed a commitment to music;
9. support the musical life of the community and encourage others to do so; and
10. are able to continue their musical learning independently.

These outcomes apply to the student who has received only the required instruction. Students who have taken elective courses in music will have developed certain specialized skills and knowledge to a higher degree. For example, the student who has played or sung in a performing group should be able to perform standard literature for his or her instrument or voice and should be able to play or sing, alone or with others, with greater skill than the student who has not had this experience. (MENC, 1986b, pp. 13–14)

Each of these sets of goals is useful for music educators and merits consideration. The establishment of broad goals is only part of the building of a music program, however. Such goals need to be implemented in class and rehearsal rooms. The form of this implementation in the schools is described and discussed in the remainder of this chapter. The presentation is divided into two parts: elementary schools (kindergarten through grades 5 or 6) and secondary schools (grades 6 or 7 through 12).

ELEMENTARY SCHOOL MUSIC PROGRAM

Most college students have only vague memories of their instruction in music back when they were eight or ten years old. In many cases they didn't receive much music instruction in school, so there isn't much to remember. In other cases the passage of ten or more years has dimmed their impression of what took place in those classes. What memories they have may consist mostly of singing songs. The experiences of the musicals and contests in high school are fresher and usually seem much more exciting. Many prospective music teachers (as well as many teachers and administrators and much of the public) associate music education largely with the high school performing groups.

This limited association and attention is indeed unfortunate. Music classes in elementary or junior high-middle schools are not only at least as important in terms of education as the performing groups, but also they can be a musically rewarding experience for everyone. The author once heard a musicologist ridicule music in the elementary schools as just the singing of songs like "The Little Red Caboose." His inaccurate perception is probably shared by quite a few people. If this view of elementary school music was ever accurate—and it may have been at one time in some places—it is certainly not the correct one today. To begin with, the content of the classes consists of much more than the singing of songs. Stepping into an elementary classroom during music, you may see students creating pieces out of sounds they find around the room; you may observe them listening to and then analyzing a short work by Mozart or Villa-Lobos or an African percussion piece; you may see the students working with classroom instruments to gain a better feeling for rhythmic or pitch patterns; and, yes, you may listen to them sing some songs, including songs in the popular idiom, folk songs, and a few art songs.

If an elementary school music class is dull, the blame falls on the teacher, who is not using the myriad of musical possibilities available to him or her.

The claim here is not that music in the elementary or junior high-middle schools operates at the same technical level as the high school performing groups. The technical level of the music is only one aspect of music, however. A well-shaped phrase and expressive performance can happen just as easily in simpler music as it can in complex works (maybe more easily). When performed expressively, William Billion's "Chester" is a stirring work, whether it is sung by a classroom of sixth graders or played by a high school band as arranged by William Schuman. Musical satisfaction should come from the expressive qualities of the music, not from its technical difficulty. Because music is music regardless of its difficulty, teaching music in the elementary schools can be musically satisfying.

The reasons for the importance of the general or classroom music program in the elementary or junior high-middle schools are very compelling. First, it is the portion of the music curriculum that involves every student. For many of them it is the *only* formal instruction they receive in music. Second, it represents the foundation on which subsequent efforts in music must be built. A child who had a hard time "carrying a tune" in the primary grades and developed doubts and fears about his or her musical ability is not a good candidate for the high school choir or band. And in later years, he or she is unlikely to be supportive of music in the schools as a voter or school board member. Therefore, music educators should work for a strong and successful program of music in the elementary schools.

In spite of its importance and its musical validity, in times of restricted school budgets classroom music is in danger of being "nibbled" away through reductions in instructional time, in number of teachers, and in funds for books and other materials. The reason for this situation is partly due to the lack of visibility for this portion of the music program. General music classes cannot (and certainly should not) enter evaluative festivals and contests in which they are rated. Nor do such classes have booster groups raising funds for them. Therefore, they do not benefit from the public awareness associated with such activities.

Partly this situation is due to a lack of awareness by school administrators of the scope and the value of the general music program. If music were just singing some songs, as they may erroneously believe, then reducing the amount of time for musical instruction merely means singing a few less songs; it's no "big deal" in their minds.

The situation is also partly due to the false ideas held by so many nonmusicians about music and talent. The popular view is this: If a person has "it" (talent), then music study is worthwhile. For most people—those with little or no talent—it doesn't matter all that much whether they receive instruction in music.

Of course, it would be wonderful if everyone supported music for all students and understood the value of music education. Maybe someday that condition will be achieved. However, for now and for the foreseeable future, teachers of general music need to work hard to put their efforts more in the public eye and to educate school administrators and the community about the nature and the value of music for all students.

One means of doing this is through performances that are both interesting and informative, or what some people call "informances." Another way is through special choirs, recorder ensembles, and similar performing groups. *If kept in proper perspective,* such groups can be important in giving this portion of the school music program the attention it deserves.

Types of Classes

Most of the music program in the elementary schools consists of classroom music; that is, music is taught to all of the children in a particular classroom at the same time for the purpose of educating them in music, not to prepare for a performance. It is required of all students and is general in nature, which implies a wide variety of activities and content. The subject matter for these classes is discussed more fully later in this chapter.

Many elementary schools offer a few music activities on an extracurricular basis. Probably the most frequent offering of this type is the glee club for students in the upper grades. Sometimes it meets during school time, but more often it utilizes a time such as noon hour or recess. Some schools offer recorder classes on this basis. Usually the method of allowing students to join such groups is by the student's expression of interest, a "selection-by-election" approach. Students are not usually auditioned for places in elementary school music groups.

Instrumental music is offered in many districts at about the fifth grade level, and in some schools a grade or two earlier or later. Many schools allow any interested student to begin instrumental study, but in some schools the size of the beginning classes is limited. In such cases, a means is found by the teachers to select the students who will be allowed to begin instrumental study. Sometimes aptitude tests are used for screening purposes, and other times reports and recommendations of the students' school music teachers are used; in some school districts students are allowed to start in a summer program, and only those students who show sufficient interest and ability are allowed to continue in the fall.

Traditionally, most of the classes consist of all wind or string instruments, but rather often families of instruments are taught together. Instrumental instruction is done by an instrumental music specialist who travels among several schools. Usually the classes meet twice a week for thirty or forty minutes. The students are excused from classroom activities according to the instrumental music teacher's schedule, since he or she usually has little flexibility in setting up the times for classes and schools. The classes tend to be small (five to fifteen students), although great size variations are found.

Amount of Time

The typical schedule for music instruction for elementary school classroom is two times a week for thirty-five minutes each time, although there is much diversity in this matter throughout America. The most comprehensive study reports seventy-six minutes per week for grades 1 through 3 and eighty-four minutes for grades 4 through 6 (National Center for Educational Statistics [NCES], 1987). Most of elective extracurricular music activities are usually on a twice-a-week basis. Some schools allow for some individualized learning activity.

Personnel Responsible for Music Instruction

Music specialists and consultants are teachers who are certified in the area of music. They majored in music in college and then took methods courses and student-teaching experience that qualified them for certification as music teachers in the elementary schools. Clearly, music specialists are strong in subject matter preparation. They are not always assigned to just one school, but, like the instrumental music teachers, sometimes travel among two or more buildings. They are responsible for only one subject: music. This has its advantages and disadvantages, as will be pointed out shortly.

The difference, if any, between music specialists and music consultants is the implication that consultants are more likely to spend their time helping classroom teachers to teach music. Actually, many people use the terms *specialist* and *consultant* interchangeably. The problem for consultants is that their advice is not requested nearly enough, except by a few teachers who are already strong in music. Teachers who are weak in music appear not to want to draw attention to that fact and, consequently, do not call on the consultant. Consultants have no administrative authority. In some cases, a consultant is responsible for a number of schools, which makes it difficult to have much personal contact with the classroom teachers. Written curriculum guides and memos must take the place of personal contacts. Sometimes consultants organize in-service instruction for teachers in a building or district. These sessions not only help the teachers to teach music better, but they also aid in improving communication and coordination among the different types of teachers.

Music supervisors are more likely to work with music specialists as administrators in the subject area of music, although the term *supervisor* is sometimes used as a synonym for *consultant*.

Classroom teachers hold a college degree in elementary education. They take about one or two music courses in their undergraduate preparation, so they have a quite limited training in music. Usually they are responsible for most of the instruction their students receive in school; the curricular areas for which they are not always responsible include physical education, art, and music.

They enjoy some advantages over music specialists in the teaching of music. They know the students in their classrooms better, and they can be more flexible about working music into the classroom routine. If ten o'clock is the best time to study the music of cowboys, then it can take place at that time. If the study of cowboy music is to be led by a music specialist, it will have to wait until the specialist's scheduled time. Furthermore, classroom teachers can integrate subject matter better since they teach most of the subjects.

Classroom teachers are clearly at a disadvantage in terms of their knowledge and ability in music. Activities that require on-the-spot musical judgments are not easy for most classroom teachers. Although they may know their twenty-five or thirty students well, they have little concept of the entire music program as it applies to other grade levels. This situation, along with the limited preparation in music, prompted the recommendation by the Teacher Education Commission of MENC that music in the elementary schools be taught by music specialists (Klotman, 1972).

Over the years the music education profession has changed its opinion about the role of classroom teachers in teaching music. In the 1940s and 1950s, a large portion of the profession promoted the idea of music teaching by classroom teachers. The 1960s saw a trend toward subject matter emphasis and a corresponding movement away from what was termed the "self-contained classroom," and so the profession retreated from the view that the classroom teacher could and should do much music teaching.

The change of attention to the subject matter content was not the only reason for less emphasis on music teaching by classroom teachers. Music educators began to realize that classroom teachers have a difficult time preparing for all the subjects they teach. Usually the subjects put off to last by classroom teachers are those that are considered "special," such as music. Also, music educators become more realistic about what could be expected of classroom teachers, who generally have little preparation in music. They realized that it is nearly impossible for classroom teachers to plan and carry out a coordinated program of music instruction for grades 1 through 6.

Although classroom teachers may not carry the brunt of the music instruction in a school system, they are still important to the success of the program in the elementary schools for the following reasons. First, there are simply not enough specialists teaching to take care of all the music instruction that is needed; classroom teachers must take up the slack, if indeed it is to be taken up.

Second, the attitude of classroom teachers toward music is important to the success of the program, even when they don't actually teach the music themselves. All teachers, whether they realize it or not, serve as behavior models for students. Elementary school students are influenced by the attitude their teachers take toward music. Children are quick to detect how their teacher feels about a subject. When a music specialist visits the classroom, a lack of interest or support from the classroom teacher can undercut what the specialist is trying to accomplish. Some classroom teachers welcome the arrival of the specialist as a break time and hurry off as fast as possible to the teachers' lounge, while sometimes others say with dismay, "It's not time for music *again,* is it?" Occasionally classroom teachers turn over unruly classes to music specialists with words such as, "They're really climbing the walls today. Lots of luck!"

Third, classroom teachers can follow up the efforts of music specialists in many ways. For example, they can have the children review a song on a day when the specialist is not in the building, hear the rest of a recording that was begun during the music lesson, and practice reading pitch or rhythm patterns. Children benefit from limited amounts of daily work in skill areas such as reading or singing, and classroom teachers are the only persons who can provide daily practice. Such follow-up is vital because, as was pointed out earlier, even when music specialists are responsible for the music instruction, the amount of time for music is quite limited.

Combination Arrangements for Instruction

It is difficult to secure up-to-date and accurate figures on who is responsible for music instruction in the elementary schools. There are many variations from state to state and district to district, and some confusion about the terminology for designating the roles of teachers. The most recent nationwide study indicates that 45 percent of all school districts are served by full-time music specialists, 39 percent by part-time specialists, and 16 percent have no music specialists (NCES, 1987). Usually the use of part-time specialists means that classroom teachers are supposed to teach some music to their students.

Content of Classroom Instruction

The material taught in music classes in the elementary classrooms is general in nature. A wide variety of topics and activities is included, and none in much depth because of the limited amount of time available. Basically students learn about music and its constituent parts (melody, rhythm, timbre, form, and so on) by becoming involved in the basic musical processes (performing, creating, and analyzing). The traditional division of the elementary school music program was into the activities associated with the basic musical processes: singing, playing instruments, rhythmic movement, creating, and reading as a part of the process of performing, and listening as the activity associated with analyzing.

The actual content included under the various classifications can be best observed in the graded music series books available for use in the elementary schools. Three publishers currently market attractive series of music books: Holt, Rinehart & Winston, Macmillan, and Silver Burdett and Ginn. The books contain many similarities, although there are a number of subtle and perhaps significant differences among them. They are filled with color illustrations, and their content is carefully prepared with the help of expert consultants to ensure accuracy. Each music series includes a teacher's edition for each grade level and a set of recordings of all the music presented in each book.

Traditionally the books were largely songbooks, but as the nature of the elementary music program has expanded, so has the variety of material in the books. The second grade books typically contain about seventy songs, of which about two-thirds are folk songs. In addition, there are listening sections, charts, creative activities, parts for classroom instruments such as autoharp, evaluation materials, ideas from the Orff and Kodály programs, the presentations of styles in music and the other arts, and suggestions for mainstreaming handicapped children. Fifth grade books contain more songs, including part songs, and present more advanced material similar to what is contained in the second grade books.

Although certainly not required for teaching music, the music series books are helpful. They are a good starting place for ideas and materials from which a teacher can build. They offer these benefits:

1. They are a source of songs and other musical activities, so a teacher is spared the effort of searching out material and ideas.

2. They provide a minimum or "bedrock" course of study in music. Often the content of the books is organized around topics or units, and a sequence of instruction is provided.

3. The teacher's edition of each book suggests teaching procedures. Reference material is included, and the songs and learning activities are thoroughly indexed.

Colored inks and other techniques are used to make the information for the teacher clear and concise.

4. Simple piano accompaniments are provided for most of the songs.

5. Ideas for incorporating classroom instruments and orchestral instruments into accompaniments are provided.

6. Pronunciation guides for all foreign language songs are included. Translations are also provided, if they are not already contained in the verses of the song.

7. The recorded performances are of a high quality. The quality of the singing, usually done by children, is also excellent. These performances provide a good model of singing for the children to copy. The musical arrangements of the songs on the recordings are tasteful, interesting, and quite authentic, with folk instruments used when appropriate.

8. They offer suggestions for extending the learning activities into other arts and other academic areas, including help for handicapped students. For teachers with the special musical approaches devised by Carl Orff and Zoltán Kodály (see Chapter 9), there are recommendations for incorporating those teaching techniques into the music instruction.

9. Many activities are suggested with which to make music classes more interesting and varied. These include scripts for plays, games, listening guides, materials for bulletin boards, recorder and guitar music, and copy masters of various items.

10. Assistance is provided in evaluating learning in music classes through appraisals of lessons and assessments of units of lessons.

To provide a better idea of what the teacher's editions are like, two pages from the Macmillan series fifth grade book are reproduced in Figure 8.1. On the pages from *Music and You* (pages 86–87), the suggestions for the teacher are printed next to the song. Since many of the users of the book are classroom teachers, curriculum information is provided in a yellow band (not visible here), as well as a phonetic pronunciation of the text. Other information is provided at the top of the page, including the key and starting note, the availability of an accompaniment, and the place in the record album where the recording can be located and other information about the recording. Cues for the teacher are printed on a reproduction of the students' page in red ink, which is not in color here, and ideas for extending the learnings are also given along with suggestions as to what to observe about the students' responses.

Two sets of materials for use in elementary school music classes are different from the basal series books. One is *Jump Right In: The Music Curriculum* by Edwin Gordon and David Woods (Chicago: G.I.A. Publications, 1984). These materials are based on Gordon's music learning theories, and they come in two parts: Learning Sequence Activities and Classroom Activities. The Learning Sequence Activi-

LESSON 4

Focus: Pitch/Major and Minor

Objectives
To aurally identify major and minor
To identify the main theme in an orchestral composition
To identify AB form in a song

Materials
Recordings: "Carol from an Irish Cabin"
"March of the Kings"
Recorded Lesson—"Playing Major and Minor"
Listening—"Farandole" from *L' Arlesienne Suite*, by Georges Bizet
"Mama, Bake the Johny Cake, Christmas Comin'"
Resonator bells or Orff Instruments
Major/Minor cue cards (or Copying Master 4–2)

1 SETTING THE STAGE

Have the students sing "Carol from an Irish Cabin" on page 79. Have them recall that the song is in minor by reviewing page 78.

2 TEACHING THE LESSON

1. Introduce "March of the Kings." Have the students:
• Listen to the song to decide if it sounds major or minor (minor) and if any melodic phrases are similar. (Phrases 1 and 2 are similar. Phrases 3 and 4 are also similar. Both sets of phrases begin in the same way, but end differently.)
• Look at the song and see that it starts and ends on F.
• Look at the tempo marking (*allegro*) and tell its English meaning. (fast)
• Identify the form. (AB)
• Listen to the song again, singing along as soon as they can.

3B
CD 2, 3

Key: F minor   Starting Pitch: F   Scale Tones: *mi, si, la, ti, do re mi fa*

SONGS IN MAJOR AND MINOR

This carol originated in a part of France called Provence (prô-väNs′). There, each year, three youths are chosen to play the kings in a procession. It is a great honor to be chosen.

• Listen for the melody in "March of the Kings." Decide if it is major or minor.   minor

March of the Kings

Piano Accompaniment on page PA 44   *French Carol*

A Allegro

Three great kings — I met at early morn, —
Ce ma - tin, J'ai ren - con - tré le train —

With all their ret - in - ue were slow - ly march - ing;
De trois grands Rois qui al - laient en voy - a - ge,

Three great kings — I met at early morn, —
Ce ma - tin, J'ai ren - con - tré le train —

were on their way to meet the new - ly born.
De trois grands Rois des - sus le grand che - min.

B

With gifts of gold brought from far a - way, —
Tout char - gés d'or les sui - vaient d'a - bord —

86

EXTENSION

CURRICULUM CONNECTION: READING

After the students have sung "March of the Kings," discuss with them the frequency of the number three in music, children's stories and literature. Have the students think of names of famous stories and music groups that involve three main characters or the number three. (for example: the Three Little Pigs, the Three Billy Goats Gruff, and so on) Have the students name (or, if necessary, tell them) the prefix which means "three". (tri) Write the prefix on the chalkboard and have the students think of words that begin with it. (for example: trio, triplets, triangle)

PRONUNCIATION

Ce	matin	J'ai	rencontré	le		train
sə	ma-taN′	zhā	rän-cōn-trä′lə			traN
De	trois	grands	Rois	qui	allaient en	voyage
də	trwä	grän	rwä	kē	ä-lä′ äN	vwä-yä′zhə
Ce	matin	J'ai	rencontré	le		train
sə	ma-taN′	zhā	rän-cōn-tra′lə			traN
De	trois	grands	Rois	dessus	le	grand chemin.
də	trwä	grän	rwä	d'su	lə	grän shə-maN′.
Tout	chargés	d'or	les	suivaient d'abord		
too	shär-zha′	dôr	lä	swē-vä′ dä-bôr′		
De	grands	guerriers et	les	gardes du		trésor
də	grän	ger-r'yä′ ā	lä	gär′də dū		tra-zôr′
Tout	chargés	d'or	les	suivaient d'abord		
too	shär-zha′	dôr	lä	swē-vä′ dä-bôr′		
De	grands	guerriers avec	leurs	boucliers.		
də	grän	ger-r'ya′ ä-vek′	lər	bōo-klē-yä′.		

86 UNIT 4

Figure 8.1   Sample pages from the teacher's edition of Music and You. *Copyright © Macmillan.*

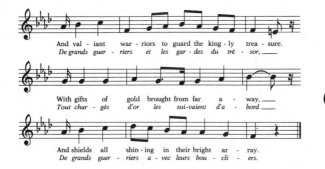

And val-iant war-riors to guard the king-ly trea-sure.
De grands guer - riers et les gar - des du tré - sor, ___

With gifts of gold brought from far a - way, ___
Tout char - gés d'or les sui - vaient d'a - bord.

And shields all shin-ing in their bright ar - ray.
De grands guer - riers a - vec leurs bou - cli - ers.

- Play the white keys from A to A. Play the white keys from C to C.
- Which is a major sound? Which is a minor sound? C to C; A to A

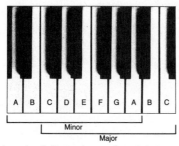

- Listen as others play. Indicate when you hear major or minor.
- Listen for major and minor in an orchestral composition that uses a melody you know.

 "Farandole," from *L'Arlésienne* by Georges Bizet (zhôrzh bē-zā')

87

MORE MUSIC TEACHING IDEAS

Have the students:
1. Sing "March of the Kings" with accompaniment played on beats 1 and 3 (♩ ♩). Use hand drums in the A section and triangles in the B section.
2. Sing the A section as a two-part canon, the second group beginning two beats later than the first. Resume unison singing in measure 9. (This effect is heard in "Farandole.")
3. Identify the syllable names of the tonal centers in major (*do*) and minor (*la,*).

LESSON 4

2. Play all the tones in the C major scale and A minor scale for aurally identifying the difference in sound. Have the students:
- Look at the diagram in the textbook.
- Listen as someone plays C to C on a keyboard (up and down) and identify this as a major sound. Then, listen as another plays from A to A and identify this as a minor sound. (Resonator bells or Orff instruments may be used.)
- Listen as several others play one of the above and show identification of each as major or minor by holding up the correct word on the cue card. You may wish to use Copying Master 4-2, at this time.
3. Introduce the listening selection, "Farandole," for practice in identifying major and minor. Have the students:
- Listen and show by raising a hand when they hear the melody of "March of the Kings" (or stand and march in place whenever they hear it.)
- Listen again and decide how the "March" sounds different the last time they hear it. (It is in major.)
- Listen again, marching in a circle on the "March" theme and standing still on the other theme. ("Dance" theme)

Reinforcing the Lesson

Review "Mama, Bake the Johnny Cake, Christmas Comin' " on page 82. Have the students:
- Sing the song.
- Decide if it is in major or minor. (major)

3 APPRAISAL

The students should be able to:
1. Show aural identification of C to C when played on bells as major and A to A as minor by showing the correct word on the cue card.
2. Show identification of the march theme in "Farandole" by marching only when it is heard.
3. Identify "March of the Kings" as AB form.

SPECIAL LEARNERS

If a class includes mainstreamed students who are unable to march in place, use a different activity for the entire class; perhaps having the students move their upper bodies to show the steady beat.

SONGBOOK

"Pat-a-Pan," page 262 (minor; seasonal; French carol)

ties present sequences for fifty-three tonal and fifty-three rhythm learning units. (Rhythm and tonal materials are presented separately.) Normally they consume five to ten minutes of the class time. The remainder of the class time is devoted to Classroom Activities. Approximately 3800 activities and techniques are contained on file cards. *Jump Right In* also includes a song collection and activity books for the students. The materials are highly structured and require a great deal of specialized and unique terminology.

Music in Education was produced in 1991 by the Yamaha Corporation. It is the first program to integrate the use of electronic keyboards, computers, software programs, and CDs. A carefully designed curriculum coordinates the various components. As is pointed out in Chapter 10, computers permit much more individual attention than books, as well as being more flexible in approach.

SECONDARY SCHOOL MUSIC PROGRAMS

No uniform national pattern exists for schools containing grades 5 or 6 through 9. There are middle schools composed of grades 5 through 8 or 6 through 8, and junior high schools consisting of grades 7 and 8 or 7 through 9. Some one-grade-level schools can also be found. In addition, there are "magnet" or special emphasis schools at both the middle and high school levels. Some of these are "schools within schools," but most are freestanding schools. Many of these magnet schools include the other arts, but not all do (Goffe, 1991).

In many ways music education in secondary schools is a very different world from its elementary school counterpart. For one thing, after the sixth or seventh grade, it involves only a small minority of the students—about one in five. Yet it is much more visible than other portions of the program. In fact, most of the public thinks first of bands and musicals as being *the* music program; the secondary school performing groups are the only portion of the program they ever hear about. Much of the program, especially at the high school level, consists of performing groups. These groups often enter evaluative or competitive festivals. Many of them have booster organizations.

As a result of these circumstances, most music teachers at the secondary school level think about their work differently from the elementary school music teachers. For example, courses of study at the secondary level are rare, in contrast to the many curriculum documents for the elementary general portions of the music program. The attention of the secondary school directors usually seems to be on performances, with limited thought given to the education of the students. The fact that the music program at the high school level involves only a minority of the students does not appear to concern most of the music teachers. Their attitude toward the rest of the school music program is not antagonistic, but it isn't all that supportive either. *Acquiescence* is probably the most accurate word to describe it.

General Music

American music education has an enviable record in terms of producing outstanding performing groups at the secondary school level, especially bands, but its accomplishments in the teaching of most students in its secondary schools are not very impressive. Part of the reason for this discrepancy between performance and nonperformance courses lies in the interest music teachers have shown in the two areas. Some teachers consider the general music class as a feeder program for high school organizations. Others see it as a recreational period in which it doesn't matter much if the students in those classes learn anything. Many teachers assigned to general music classes would rather be directing high school groups; they simply have not given general music classes much attention and thought. As a result, quite a number of junior high-middle schools have reduced or eliminated general music. In the nine years from 1973 to 1982, when school enrollments were increasing significantly, enrollments in general music fell significantly (MENC, 1990).

Accurate data are hard to come by for music in middle schools, but the trend seems to be downward. Many middle schools have relegated general music to a set of "exploratory" courses that all sixth or seventh grade students (except in many cases those in instrumental music) take in one course that is six or nine weeks long. That course is the total middle school music experience for most students. This exploratory rotation of electives, sometimes called the "wheel," provides a very limited education in music and has caused major problems for performing groups at the middle school level. The situation reached the point in 1990 where MENC declared music in middle schools to be one of its priorities for action.

In some school systems the general music course in the junior high-middle school is the first instruction in music the students receive from a music specialist. In other school systems the students have a strong background in music because of the elementary school experiences.

The size of general music classes varies. Often they are the same size as other academic classes, but in some cases they contain sixty or more students.

The content of the general music classes at the middle school level differs somewhat from music instruction at the elementary level in terms of the attention given the various aspects of music instruction. Although some singing and other music-making activities are continued, more time and effort is devoted to listening and analyzing. There are at least two reasons for the increased emphasis on listening in general music classes. One is that many of the boys are undergoing a change of voice, and singing is not as easy or satisfying during this transition. A second and more important reason is that after the students finish their education, the main contact most of them will have with music will be as listeners, not as singers or instrumentalists. Therefore, music teachers need to help students to improve their skill in listening to music.

Although listening should receive more attention in middle school general music classes, singing and other types of music making should still be continued. As is pointed out in Chapter 6, singing and playing instruments can contribute

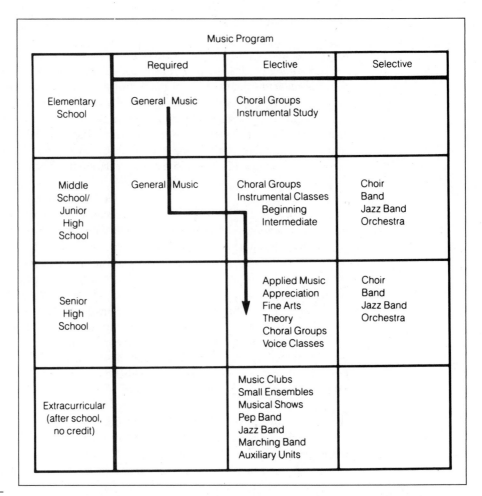

Figure 8.2   *Music programs at American schools.*

much to the students' sensitivity awareness in music. General music should not become a class in which students only listen to and discuss music.

Elective Courses

In addition to the general music classes for most of the seventh grade students, specific courses are offered on an elective basis. These electives include band, choral groups, orchestra, and a host of extracurricular activities. Figure 8.2 shows the nature of the music program at the three levels found in American schools.

The most recent national data on the elective and general music courses in the high schools are as follows:

Course	Students enrolled	*Percent of total* *high school enrollment*
Band	1,111,000	8.8
Orchestra	86,000	0.7
Instrumental ensembles	52,000	0.4
Instrumental classes	190,000	1.5
Chorus, choir, glee club	1,061,000	8.4
General music	61,000	0.5
Appreciation	99,000	0.8
Theory/Composition	72,000	0.6
Total	2,732,000	21.7

Source: National Center for Educational Statistics (1987). *Public school district policies in selected aspects of arts and humanities instruction.* (Washington, DC: U.S. Department of Education), p. 55.

Although the exactness of the various figures may be questioned, they offer a good general idea of the situation in the early 1980s. Several important conclusions can be drawn from these data: (1) The enrollment in high school music courses is heavily in band and choral music. (2) Band enrollment is about twelve times larger than that for orchestra, reflecting the fact that only about one high school in five offers orchestra. (3) The enrollment in general music, appreciation, and theory courses make up only 8.49 percent of all the music enrollments, leaving 91.51 percent in performance groups. Clearly, the music curriculum at the high school level is overwhelmingly in performing organizations.

Although performing groups dominate the music program in America's high schools, music educators should not forget about theory, appreciation, and fine arts courses. They should do what they reasonably can to bring the performance and nonperformance aspects of the program into a better balance. Often this balance can be helped by seeing to it that some nonperformance courses are offered in the school curriculum and then promoting them among the students. If teachers have the opportunity to teach such a course, they should devote as much effort to the course as they do their top performing groups. Finally, music educators should try to educate the school administration and community about the values of nonperformance courses in the music program.

Some historical background is needed to understand why secondary school music is so performance-oriented. The great leap forward in secondary school enrollments occurred between the years 1910 and 1940. During that period a person's chances of attending high school increased from one in ten to three in four (U.S. Dept. of Health, Education, and Welfare, 1970). This increase meant that many of the students going to high school were not college-bound, so a greater variety of courses were needed in the curriculum. Also, attitudes changed somewhat about the values of studying subjects other than the traditional academic ones. Because school music at the secondary level expanded rapidly, there were few teachers trained to teach music at the secondary school level. Therefore, schools often turned to professional musicians, a trend that was greatly boosted by the unemployment of the early 1930s. These former professional musicians, naturally, worked with their performing groups in much the same way as a director of a professional organization. The period when the band or choir met was called a "rehearsal," and the purpose of the band or choir was to present polished and perfected performances. The teacher was designated the "director," a term more familiar to professional musicians. So music became the only curricular area in which "directors" conduct "rehearsals" instead of teachers teaching classes.

Many of the professional musicians who entered the teaching field made valuable contributions to music education. Even today the limited opportunities for making a living as a performer have turned many persons toward teaching in the schools. Common interests bind the professional musicians and music educators together, and the teaching profession needs capable and sensitive musicians. What should be realized, however, is that whatever is good for a professional organization is not always the best for a school performing group. Because the two groups exist for different purposes, they should be approached somewhat differently.

There are several good reasons for continuing performing groups in the secondary school curriculum. One is that students learn by doing and experiencing. Students who go through the effort of learning their parts and rehearsing with the group know a musical work much more thoroughly than students who only listened to it. Many a student who had an initial lack of interest in a piece of music has ended up liking it after working on it.

Another point in favor of performing groups is that they fulfill teenage needs for recognition and activity. In most of their other school courses, students sit passively. Music is one area in which they can truly participate. Preparing music for a performance motivates them, as well as offers them a chance for some recognition.

A third point in favor of performing groups is that they are well established in the school curriculum. Teachers are trained in teaching performing groups, and materials are available. Before discarding such achievements, something of greater value should be found to replace them.

What appears to be needed in the future is (1) a building up of the non-performance courses and (2) an evolution (not a revolution) toward more educationally valid performing groups. Ways of increasing the amount and type of learning in performing groups, which are beyond the scope of this book, are presented in the author's *Teaching Music in the Secondary Schools,* Fourth edition.

Types of Performing Groups

Not all secondary school students can profit equally from music instruction. Students want and need music instruction that is suited to their abilities and interests. When enough enrollment permits, groups at different levels of ability should be offered. There can be a choir for the more interested and talented students, and a chorus for the less able and interested. The same idea holds true for instrumental groups. Such an arrangement is consistent with the democratic tenet of equal opportunity. Teachers need to guard against slighting the less talented group. The education given students in a chorus is just as important as the education given the students in the top choir; only the level at which the learning takes place is different.

Small Ensembles. A weakness of music education at the secondary school level is its lopsided emphasis on large ensembles. Most music educators realize that performing in small ensembles is a valuable experience for students. They gain independence by being the only performer on a part, and small ensemble work engenders interest and good musicianship. In addition, there is a rich literature for combinations involving strings and groups such as woodwind quintets and brass ensembles.

At least three factors discourage small ensembles in the schools. To begin with, it is hard to work up much public enthusiasm for a woodwind quintet or horn trio, which is not true for bands or choral groups. Second, the time that teachers can devote to small ensembles is limited. Their schedules are filled with classes and large ensemble rehearsals. Few school systems can afford to hire a teacher for classes of four or five students. Third, the amount of time available to students for small ensembles is limited. Very few students have time in their school schedules for more than one music class per day, and that class usually is a large ensemble. Most small ensembles are formed for purposes of performing at a contest, and they meet only a few times with a teacher.

These problems do not erase the fact that small ensemble experience is highly desirable. Some teachers arrange for several small ensembles to rehearse at the same time in adjacent rooms so that they can circulate among the groups. In some situations the better performers form an ensemble. Because they learn their parts more quickly than the other students, they can be excused from large ensemble rehearsal once or twice a week to rehearse small ensemble music.

Orchestras. For a variety of reasons orchestras have been far surpassed in enrollment by bands. This is a truly unfortunate situation, for two reasons. First, the orchestral literature is much richer than that for bands. Very few of the "name" composers throughout music history have written for bands. Except for some contemporary works, bands must play pieces written for the educational market or transcriptions, which are not usually as effective as the original works. The wind band is slowly acquiring some good contemporary literature of its own, and possibly in fifty years the problem of good literature will not be so serious. Second, the playing opportunities after high school for interested amateurs lie overwhelmingly in orchestras, which use only a limited number of winds.

When speaking candidly, many band directors give three reasons for not offering string instruction: (1) It might take potentially good players away from the band. The result might be two mediocre groups instead of one good organization. (2) There is no one competent enough to teach strings in the district. (3) The band director has no time for any more classes. The first reason may have some truth to it in school districts with enrollments of less than 1000 for grades 7 through 12. However, some small districts have a good band and a good orchestra. The excuse of a lack of string teaching ability is not valid. Band directors who are clarinet players do not hesitate teaching brass instruments, at least at the beginning and intermediate levels.

The matter of teacher time must be faced. It is not possible to get something for nothing. Fortunately, school-quality string instruments cost about the same as wind instruments, and often they can be rented from music merchants, in which cases an investment by the school district is not required. During the first year or two in which a string program is started, only a small amount of additional teacher time is needed. When the program reaches to all grades, the program adds about one-fourth as much instructional time as the winds require.

Marching Bands. The marching band has commendable features. It is good public relations for the music department. Many people see the band only at a football game or street parade, and that is their only contact with the school music program. Its members achieve recognition, school spirit is fostered, and good feelings are generated all around as the colorful groups parade by. What could anyone have against something that gives so many people harmless enjoyment and impresses them favorably with the school music program?

The problem is that in some communities the marching band has dominated the music program in the school district; in some high schools the marching band has become almost the entire music program. In such instances the result is a limited music education for a small number of students and just about no music education for the vast majority of the students.

The problem has been intensified over the past decade in many places because of the growth of marching band contests and the increasing popularity of the corps style of marching. Aside from its technical features, such as style of step, corps-style bands usually learn only one show each year, and they perform this show for every appearance. Clearly this one show provides the students with a very restricted musical experience. Many of the appearances are at marching band contests, with some bands entering five or more contests each fall. The evaluation of bands at these contests is based largely on nonmusical factors, and a correlation has been observed by many people between the size of the group (band members and auxiliary units) and the ratings received. One study of high school bands uncovered the fact that many students liked the competition and potential recognition but realized that they learned much more in a concert band. Even many of the directors of successful contest bands freely admitted that the experience has little to do with educating students in music (Rogers, 1982). The values claimed for the marching activity, both at contests and at football games, were the promotion of the band and character building and recognition for the students— reasons that hark back to the topic of the nonmusical values of music discussed in Chapter 1.

What can music educators who direct bands do about the situation? In most American communities today the marching band is so much a part of the scene that it is unrealistic to suggest that it be discontinued, and probably that would not be a good idea anyway. Teachers can begin by bringing the attention devoted to the marching band into proportion with that given other aspects of the music program. In some cases this adjustment may mean reducing (over a period of a

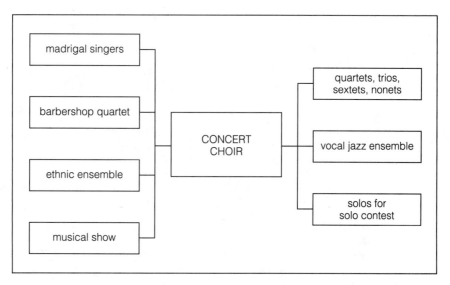

Figure 8.3   *Concert choir and related groups.*

couple of years) the number of marching appearances or contests entered. It may mean simplifying the marching shows in terms of the routines the students are expected to learn. Truthfully, most football fans cannot tell the difference between a complicated and a simple band show (or maybe they don't care). A third action that will make the teachers' lives a little easier is to have someone else oversee the auxiliary units—flag bearers, rifle corps, pom-pom unit, and so on. Other teachers or people in the community can work with these groups, and music teachers will have more time for teaching music, which is what they were trained to do.

Jazz Bands and Swing Choirs. Should "specialized" performing groups such as jazz bands, madrigal singers, and swing choirs be included in the secondary school curriculum on the same basis as band, orchestra, choir, and general music? Certainly such groups should be offered when possible, but they should be operated as adjuncts to the larger groups. For example, jazz band membership should be made available only to the members of the concert band or to those who have been members for two or more years. This principle is strongly promoted by MENC (1986a). Figures 8.3 and 8.4 present charts for band and choir that depict the other related groups ancillary to the main organization.

The reason for this recommendation concerns the quality of the education the students receive in music. A student's musical education is limited by his or her premature selection of one specialized area before becoming educated to some degree about a larger world of music.

In some schools such specialized groups have received most of the attention of the teacher and the public, and the larger group has been neglected. For example, one prestigious suburban high school let its concert band deteriorate noticeably while a steel band was receiving most of the director's attention.

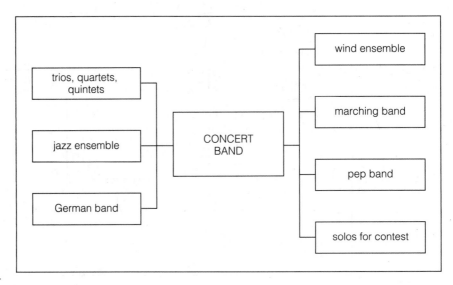

Figure 8.4   *Concert band and related groups.*

Music teachers in many states are certified for all school grades. Even when not certified for all levels, they should realize that they are a part of a large and varied program of instruction. If music is to be solidly in the schools, it needs to be a coordinated and planned effort from kindergarten through grade 12. Both the students and music teachers will benefit when this is done.

Questions

1. Are the three general classifications of goals (skills, understandings, and attitudes) equally important?

2. From your experience, to which general classification of goal is most of the time in music classes and rehearsals devoted?

3. Why is the general music program in the elementary schools an important and essential part of the school music program? Why does the general music program sometimes face tough going when it comes to funding?

4. What is the composition of a typical music program at the elementary school level in terms of type of teacher, instruction offered, amount of time, students involved, and materials used?

5. What are the advantages of having music in the elementary classroom taught by a music specialist?

6. What are the advantages of having music in the elementary classroom taught by the classroom teacher?

7. What are the benefits of using one of the graded music series books?

8. In what ways does the music program at the secondary school level differ from the music program at the elementary school level?

9. How does the content of the general music program at the middle school level differ from its counterpart at the elementary school level?

10. What are some reasons why music course offerings in American high schools are so heavily weighted toward performing groups?

11. Why should small ensemble experiences be provided for students in high school performing groups?

12. Why should string orchestra be included in the school music curriculum?

13. Why are concert band, orchestra, and choir the "core" of the performing groups in the secondary school music curriculum?

Projects

1. Examine the three sets of goals listed on pages 93–94.
   a. Identify the ones in the list from *Music in General Education* that are similar to ones in the list from *The School Music Program: Description and Standards*.
   b. Classify the ten outcomes in *The School Music Program: Description and Standards* list under the classifications of skills, understandings, and attitudes.
   c. Place each of the outcomes in the list from *The School Music Program: Description and Standards* into three categories (very important/important/less important) according to your views about what students should gain from their school music instruction.

2. Think about the schools you attended. Either during a visit home or by writing to someone you know who lives there, find out the following:
   a. Is elementary general music taught by music specialists or classroom teachers?
   b. How much time is allotted each week for general music in the elementary schools?
   c. What music courses are offered in the high school curriculum?

References

Ernst, K. E., & Gary, C. L. (Eds.). (1965). *Music in general education*. Reston, VA: Music Educators National Conference.

Goffe, J. (1991). *Music programs in performing arts high schools: Current status and implications for future development*. Unpublished doctoral dissertation, University of Florida.

Klotman, R. H. (Ed.). (1972). *Teacher education in music: Final report*. Reston, VA: Music Educators National Conference.

Music Educators National Conference. (1986a). *Guidelines for performances of school music groups: Expectations and limitations*. Reston, VA: Author.

Music Educators National Conference. (1986b). *The school music program: Description and standards* (2nd ed.). Reston, VA: Author.

Music Educators National Conference. (1990). *Data on music education*. Reston, VA: Author.

National Center for Educational Statistics. (1987). *Public school district policies in selected aspects of arts and humanities instruction*. Washington, DC: U.S. Department of Education.

Rogers, G. L. (1982). *Attitudes of high school band directors, band members, parents, and principals toward marching band contests*. Unpublished doctoral dissertation, Indiana University.

Soundpost, 3 (8) (Spring 1992), p. 9.

U.S. Department of Health, Education, and Welfare. (1970). *Digest of educational statistics*. Washington, DC: U.S. Government Printing Office.

CHAPTER 9

International Curriculum Developments

A*merica* has a long tradition of adopting artistic ideas from other countries. For example, furniture makers during the eighteenth century adopted stylistic ideas from the Orient, resulting in what is today called "Chinese Chippendale." Until well into the twentieth century, painters and composers felt that a period of study in Europe was a prerequisite to a successful career. However, Americans were not so quick to adopt ideas about education from other countries. Until the past few decades, educators felt that America's great experiment in universal education had little to learn from the educational practices of other countries. In fact, after the end of World War II, it seemed as if many other countries were adopting American educational ideas as fast as they could.

Music educators are different in this respect, perhaps as a result of their artistic heritage. Beginning in the 1960s, they have shown interest in three significant approaches or "methods" from other countries: the Orff *Schulwerk* from Germany, the Kodály concept of music education from Hungary, and the Talent Education program of Suzuki in Japan. Also there has been renewed interest in the methods of the Swiss music educator Jaques-Dalcroze. The reason for the interest of American music teachers in these four programs is not hard to pinpoint: Each has produced highly impressive results with its students. It is the results, not clever promotional schemes, that have attracted the attention of music teachers.

While these four approaches are certainly not the only ones to be found in other countries, they are the ones that have come to the attention of American music educators. Prospective music teachers should be familiar with the main features of each of them.

DALCROZE APPROACH

Development and Background

Émile Jaques-Dalcroze (1865–1950) began teaching music shortly before the turn of the century. Music study at that time was divided into segmented courses such as harmony, sight-singing, form and analysis, and so on. Jaques-Dalcroze* noticed many students knew music only in an intellectual way:

> When he asked his students to write down chords during their harmony classes he discovered that they were not really hearing what they had written, and that for most

---

*His approach is usually referred to by only the second half of his name.

of them harmony was simply a matter of mathematics. It became clear to him that the traditional method of training musicians concentrated on the intellect to the detriment of the senses, and failed to give students a valid *experience* of the basic elements of music sufficiently early in their studies. (Dobbs, 1968, p. 13)

He also noticed that students had trouble performing rhythmic patterns but had no problem with rhythmic motor activities such as walking. From these observations he concluded that people instinctively have musical rhythm but do not transfer these instincts to music. He started experimenting with this idea by having students walk to music in different tempos. Slowly more parts of the body were asked to respond to music. In this way he developed an approach for learning music that has three main parts: (1) *eurhythmics*—the rhythmic response to music; (2) *solfège*—singing with syllables; and (3) improvisation.

The idea of responding physically to music was revolutionary in Geneva in 1902. (The students in Jaques-Dalcroze's classes were barefooted and wore comfortable clothing!) He soon left the Geneva Conservatory and opened his own studio and continued to experiment. Later a group of Geneva businessmen set up a school for him in Hellerau, Germany. Between 1910 and 1914, interest in his method grew greatly. Among the famous people who attended his classes were the English playwright George Bernard Shaw, the Polish patriot and pianist Paderewski, Rachmaninoff, and dancers like Martha Graham and Ted Shawn. The outbreak of World War I in 1914 caused him to leave Germany and to establish the Institut Jaques-Dalcroze in Geneva, which is now a part of the Conservatory of Music.

Although Jaques-Dalcroze felt that his method could not be understood only by reading about it, he did write down some of his exercises. In *Rhythm, Music and Education* he presents a list of twenty-two kinds of exercise for each of the three branches of his approach under these headings: "Rhythmic Movement," "Solfège or Aural Training," and "Piano Improvisation." The approach depends almost entirely on personal instruction, however.

The Dalcroze approach was introduced in the United States in about 1915. The public schools could not provide time or space for it to be taught in its authentic form, which was the only way Jaques-Dalcroze wanted it taught. However, some teachers adapted his procedures, and in other cases teachers were influenced by the approach without being aware of it. The use of "walking" and "running" as designations for quarter and eighth notes is one common example in the elementary schools. By the 1930s, a number of college music schools or physical education departments were requiring courses in *eurhythmics,* the term often used for Dalcroze-like instruction. The interest in it seemed to level off at that point and then decline. A modest renewal of interest in it has taken place since 1970. About twenty colleges offer some instruction in the approach, with four of them giving a Dalcroze certificate.

Characteristics of the Dalcroze Approach

1. A physical response to music is basic to the Dalcroze approach, and it somewhat dominates the early lessons. This portion is the one for which it is best known and is called *eurhythmics*—a word derived from the Greek, meaning "good rhythm or flow." The purpose of the movement is to create rhythmic sensitivity in the students by making them feel musical rhythm in their entire bodies. Musical concepts are also reinforced through physical movements. Sometimes the students begin with a representation of an idea, such as something getting louder. The bodily movement to represent the idea, which should be one familiar in life, is tried first without music. For example, it might consist of walking with the steps becoming more and more energetic. Next the student listens to music in which a crescendo is easily heard. Then the movement is synchronized with the music. The term *crescendo* may follow the experience of the idea through bodily movement, and later the musical symbol for it may be presented. In more advanced classes students may use the idea in notation and improvisation.

The physical movements are not predetermined, but rather are the spontaneous products of each individual. Therefore, great differences are usually seen in the responses of a group of students to the same music. However, the students do learn a "grammar of gestures" in a way similar to that of a conductor. The classes usually involve some group interaction, as well as individual response. Although some ballet dancers studied with Jaques-Dalcroze, he insisted that he was a teacher of music, not dance. There are, however, many consonant ideas between modern dance training and eurhythmics.

Two rhythmic exercises are cited here from an adaptation of Jaques-Dalcroze's book to give a clearer idea of the type of activity that takes place in the classes.

Exercise 1. Following the Music, Expressing Tempo and Tone Quality

The teacher at the piano improvises music to which the pupils march (usually in a circle) beating the time with their arms (3/4, 5/8, 12/8, etc.) as an orchestra leader conducts, and stepping with their feet the note values (that is, quarter notes are indicated by normal steps, eighth notes by running steps, half notes by a step and a bend of the leg, a dotted eighth and a sixteenth by a skip, etc.). The teacher varies the expression of the playing, now increasing or decreasing the intensity of tone, now playing more slowly or more quickly; and the pupils "follow the music" literally, reproducing in their movements the exact pattern and structure of her improvisation.

Exercise 9. Independence of Control

This exercise is one in polyrhythm, the pupil expressing several rhythms at the same time. He may perhaps beat three-four time with the left arm and four-four with the right at the same time walking twelve-eight with the feet. There are many variations of this though in the beginning pupils find it sufficiently difficult to beat two with one arm and three with the other, especially since each arm must "remember," so to speak, the accent which falls on the first beat of its own measure. Another form of this exercise is to have the pupils march one measure while beating time for another; as three with the arms and four with the feet. These are worked out mathematically at first but soon the pupils learn to keep in their muscular and mental consciousnesses the pulse of the two rhythms simultaneously. (Pennington, 1925, pp. 14–26)

2. The second main branch of the Dalcroze approach is solfège, in which the familiar pitch syllables are used, but *do* is always C, *di* is C#, and so on. Jaques-Dalcroze thought that solfège singing developed the ability to listen to and remember tonal patterns. Singing and hand positions for designating the level of pitches of the scale are used in learning solfège, and these activities precede experience with notation.

Much emphasis is placed on inner hearing—the ability to imagine music in the mind. Students in Dalcroze classes sing intervals and songs with syllables. Some of the measures in the song are sung aloud, and others are sung silently in the mind.

> A melody would be placed on the blackboard with some empty measures which the student would be expected to fill in, improvising, as he sang the melody for the first time.

> Another exercise involved writing a melody on the blackboard and as the students sang it through, each phrase was erased upon completion of this initial singing. A student would then be asked to sing the entire melody by memory. (Becknell, 1970, p. 13)

Reading music and working with notation is a part of solfège training, but only after a solid foundation of experiences with music has been built. Notation is always related to sound. For example, tones may be played on the piano, and the young students identify them by standing beside cards laid on the floor containing the numbers 1 through 8. Rhythm may initially be notated by marking patterns on large sheets of paper with dots and dashes to represent the various lengths of notes or rests.

3. Improvising is the third main branch of the Dalcroze approach to musical training. It is an integral part of eurhythmics and solfège activities. Jaques-Dalcroze believed that each student should have the experience of expressing his or her own musical ideas.

Improvisation is begun on percussion instruments or with the voice. Sometimes a child is given one measure to which he or she improvises a response, all the while maintaining the basic beat. Spoken commands or signals are given while improvisation is going on. This practice makes the students listen carefully and encourages skill development. For example, while the students are executing a rhythmic pattern with their feet, they may be asked to do a contrasting pattern with their arms.

After the students have successfully improvised with their voices and on percussion instruments, they begin to improvise on the piano. Improvising at the piano is stressed for advanced students and teachers.

ORFF SCHULWERK

Development and Background

Carl Orff (1895–1982) was a recognized contemporary composer. His best-known works are *Carmina Burana* and *Catulli Carmina*. He began the *Schulwerk* (which in German simply means "school work") with Dorothea Günther in Munich in 1924. At the time, education in Europe was heavily influenced by Jaques-Dalcroze, and there were numerous schools for gymnastics and dance. What made *Schulwerk* different was that its main interest was in music. The school grew and in due course had an ensemble of dancers and an orchestra, with the players and dancers being interchangeable. The group toured Europe and attracted much favorable attention.

During World War II the school was destroyed and the instruments lost. Orff did not renew his educational activities until 1948, when he was asked by the Bavarian radio to present a program of music for children. The request caused him to rethink his views on music education. The earlier school with Günther had been for teenagers, but now Orff realized that the educational process should start much earlier with young children.

> I began to see things in the right perspective. "Elemental" was the password, applicable to music itself, to the instruments, to forms of speech and movement. What does it mean? The Latin word *elementarius,* from which it is derived, means "pertaining to the elements, primeval, basic." What, then, is elemental music? Never music alone, but music connected with movement, dance, and speech—not to be listened to, meaningful only in active participation. Elemental music is pre-intellectual, it lacks great form, it contents itself with simple sequential structures, ostinatos, and miniature rondos. It is earthy, natural, almost a physical activity. (Orff, 1990, p. 143)

The reborn *Schulwerk* was a success, and what started as a single broadcast was continued for five years. Between 1950 and 1954, the five basic volumes of *Schulwerk* music were published. Regular courses in *Schulwerk* were started in 1949 at the Mozarteum in Salzburg, Austria, under the direction of Gunild Keetman. The Orff Institute was established in Salzburg in 1963.

Although five books of Orff's music for children are available, he intended them to serve only as models for what the children can do. In no sense do they constitute a course of study or standard repertoire. The emphasis on improvising has also discouraged the use of music notation. The main purpose of writing music down is to retain a piece once it has been worked out.

Schulwerk does not have a set course of study; "those who look for a method or ready-made system are rather uncomfortable with *Schulwerk,*" Orff has stated (Orff, 1990, p. 138). The lack of an established set of procedures leads to quite different actions and results under the heading of Orff *Schulwerk*. Orff himself has commented on the situation in these words, "Unfortunately, it [*Schulwerk*] has often been misinterpreted, exploited, and falsified to the point of caricature" (Orff, 1990, p. 138).

Orff's interest in "elemental" music may strike many readers as a bit unusual. It derives from a theory about human development that states that children's musical development roughly corresponds to the development of music. According to this theory, rhythm preceded melody, and melody preceded harmony. Whether one finds this theory agreeable or not, it is not necessary to adopt it in order to teach aspects of *Schulwerk*.

Orff's ideas have been studied by many American music educators. By 1980, about two-thirds of the elementary music specialists in the United States had participated in workshops on *Schulwerk,* with nearly one-fourth of these teachers having four or more weeks of special training in it (Hoffer, 1981). Several trial programs were conducted in school districts around the United States in the 1960s and 1970s. *Schulwerk* has also been adapted for use with handicapped and exceptional children.

Characteristics of Schulwerk .

1. Speech rhythms are an important part of the early instruction in *Schulwerk*. The children chant out rhymes, calls, and traditional sayings in a vigorous rhythmic fashion. For instance, short phrases for chanting can be derived from the pattern of the students' names (Kraus, 1990) as in the following example:

Meter and accent are also introduced in speech patterns. The students sometimes chant a phrase or sentence in canon—a spoken round. As the children become more adept at speech patterns, they are introduced through them to phrasing, dynamics, and styles such as legato and staccato; simple forms such as rondo can also be introduced through speech patterns. Speech patterns are often combined with patterns of body rhythms: clapping; snapping the fingers; and *patschen* (thigh slaps), which are characteristic in *Schulwerk*. A pattern of clapping and thigh slapping can become a theme, for example, and it can be varied, repeated, performed antiphonally, or become the theme for a rondo.

2. Singing experiences following the speech pattern work, which adheres to Orff's idea that melody follows rhythm. Singing at the early stages contains many short phrases sung back and forth between teacher and students and between students. Usually the singing is accompanied by instruments and/or body rhythms.

The first interval learned is *sol-mi,* the descending minor third. Unlike the Dalcroze method, however, the syllables are movable, not fixed. Words are usually added to these simple two-note phrases, as in this example:

"No. 8" from Carl Orff and Gunild Keetman, *Music for Children, Volume I: Pentatonic,* English adaption by Doreen Hall and Arnold Waltzer (Mainz: B. Schott's Sohne, 1960), p. 92. Used by permission of European American Distributors Corporation, sole U.S. agent for B. Schott's Sohne.

The intervals are introduced in a certain sequence. After *sol* and *mi* comes *la*, then *re*, and then *do*, which completes a pentatonic scale. The major and minor scales are taught, but not until later. Orff favors the pentatonic scale because he thinks it is more natural. Also, half steps with their strong melodic tendencies are avoided when improvising, a topic that will be mentioned shortly.

3. Movement is an important part of *Schulwerk* as conceived by Orff, but it is not utilized as much in American adaptations of it. Orff's views about the value and purpose of bodily movement are similar to those of Jaques-Dalcroze. The natural, untrained actions of children are the basis for movement. Running, skipping, hopping, and other physical movements are part of the students' musical development. Generally the movements are free and individual, and are intended to express the music.

4. Improvisation is central to *Schulwerk,* and it is found in all its activities—speech, movement, singing, and instrument playing. The initial efforts in improvising are highly structured. The child is given a limited number of pitches to use in creating a short melodic or rhythmic fragment of a specified length. Often these first efforts involve only *sol* and *mi* for one or two measures. As the students gain experience in improvising, more pitches are added and the patterns are made longer and more complex. Many times short introductions and codas are added to pieces, and many pieces employ an ostinato.

5. Instrument playing is an important aspect of *Schulwerk*. Not just any instrument is acceptable in the program. Orff wanted the children's ears to become accustomed to the sound of quality instruments. Furthermore, he wanted the instruments to be easy to play, and he favored those that had a "primitive appeal." So he had simple mallet instruments constructed that are capable of carrying the melody: xylophones, metallophones, and glockenspiels in various sizes. Later, instruments such as flutes and gambas were added. Some percussion were also used. After the original instruments were mostly destroyed in World War II, Orff worked with Klauss Becker, who developed the Studio 49 instruments found in many Orff classes today and shown in Figure 9.1. Not only do these instruments have a good tone quality and come in several sizes, they are useful in improvising because any unneeded bars can be removed temporarily so that they will not be struck accidentally by the student. The piano is not used for most works. *Schulwerk* instruments are not considered toys, but rather as an important means for making music. Most of the playing is done from memory or is improvised, which frees the student from the demand to read music.

6. The reading of music comes only after several years of training. Even then its main function is to preserve improvisations and arrangements.

7. Orff's music, and the music used and created in *Schulwerk,* has a strong folklike character. It contains short, energetic melodic ideas, many ostinatos, simple harmonies, and at times an almost primitive quality.

The following labels accompany the figure:

1	Kettle drums	9	Soprano xylophone	17	Castanets
2	Bass drum	10	Box rattle	18	Hanging cymbals
3	Tambours (hand drum)	11	Alto glockenspeil	19	Claves
4	Bass xylophone	12	Alto-soprano glockenspeil	20	Wood block
5	Alto metallophone	13	Bell spray	21	Finger cymbal
6	Alto xylophone	14	Felt head beater	22	Sleigh bells
7	Alto-soprano xylophone	15	Soprano glockenspeil		
8	Gourd	16	Triangles		

Figure 9.1   *Studio 49 instruments.*

KODÁLY APPROACH

Development and Background

Like Orff, Zoltán Kodály (1882–1967) was a recognized composer. *Háry János* is his best-known work, but he has many successful compositions. He was a friend and colleague of Béla Bartók, and he worked with him on studying and collecting Hungarian folk songs. He was also greatly interested in the music education of children. "No one is too great to write for children," he wrote. "Quite the opposite—one should strive to be worthy of this task" (Kraus, 1990, p. 80). Living up to his word, Kodály composed about twenty books of music for school students. They begin with very simple material for preschool children and continue through four-part works of great difficulty. In addition, he guided his native Hungary in the establishment of an exemplary program of music education in its schools.

World War II and the Nazi occupation of Hungary delayed the implementation of Kodály's educational ideas until after 1945. A new educational system was being established, and in spite of its political limitations, the situation provided an unusual opportunity to design a new music program. Education in Hungary was state controlled and had a heritage of strict academic training, so it was possible to institute a strong national program. Today most children in the elementary schools of Hungary receive two forty-five-minute periods of music each week. Through the fourth grade music is taught by classroom teachers, who have had much more collegiate training in music than their American counterparts. From grades 5 through 8 music is taught by specialists.

The portion of Hungary's music education program that has especially impressed foreign observers is the 130 "Music Primary Schools." These schools are similar to other elementary schools, except for one important difference: The students receive one hour of musical instruction each day from a music specialist. Parents make application to these schools on behalf of their children, who are then selected on the basis of musical tests (Carder, 1990). Therefore, the Music Primary Schools are not typical elementary schools. A carefully devised course of study in music is followed rigorously in these schools. The overall plan for the presentation of topics in grade 1 appears in Figure 9.2. The curriculum prescribes the sequence of instruction, and the textbooks provide a minimum amount of material. Each teacher then develops at the beginning of the year a syllabus that states when the material will be studied during the year. Some activities are left up to the teacher's interest and abilities.

The Music Primary School program began to attract international attention after presentations by Hungarian music educators at conferences of the International Society of Music Education in 1958, 1961, and especially 1964, when Kodály himself addressed the conference. Since the mid-1960s, American music educators have traveled to Hungary to observe or study the program, and a number of Hungarian music teachers have taught in the United States. By 1980, nearly half of the elementary music specialists in the United States had taken workshops in the Kodály approach, and over 12 percent had had more than four weeks of training in it (Hoffer, 1981).

FIRST GRADE CURRICULUM
OF THE HUNGARIAN MUSIC PRIMARY SCHOOLS (1978)

I. Musical Materials
  Singing
    45–50 rhymes, children's game songs, composed songs, patriotic songs (required material indicated)
    Kodály, *333 Singing Exercises* (selections as appropriate)
    Kodály, *Pentatonic Music, Vol. I* (selections)
  Music Listening
    Performances by the teacher of children's and folk songs
    Recordings (or live performances) of significant portions of
      Bartók, *For Children*
      Kodály, *Children's and Women's Choruses*
      L. Mozart, *Children's Symphony*
      Kodály, *Pentatonic Music, Vol. I.*
    Recordings of folk instruments and field recordings of folk music performances

II. Musical Knowledge and Skills
  Steady beat
  Melodic rhythm
  Quarter note
  Paired eighth notes
  Quarter rest
  Half note
  Half rest
  Duple meter (simple)
  Bar line
  Double bar line
  Repeat sign
  Extended pentatonic scale notes (*so mi la do re la so do'*) with solfège, hand signs, staff placement, reading, and writing in the solfège system
  Perception and discrimination of different timbres: vocal/instrumental, child's/adult's, male/female, piano/recorder/metallofon
  Musical ensembles (chorus/orchestra)
  Dynamics: fast, slow, moderate
  Motives from children's songs
  Repetition
  Ostinato
  Playing of simpler pentatonic motives on the recorder

III. Distribution of class time
  Required material: approximately 85 classes
  Supplementary material: approximately 43 classes
    Of this: 60% singing activities
          10% listening activities
          30% cognitive activities

IV. Behavioral objectives (corresponding to above material)

Figure 9.2   *Overall plan for presentation of topics in grade 1.*

Kodály's manual for Hungarian teachers has been translated into English, and much of the music he wrote for children is available in the United States. Several American music educators have developed materials based on Kodály's ideas. One of the first to do this was Mary Helen Richards; Lorna Zemke, Denise Bacon, Lois Chosky, and others have followed. Some Kodály techniques are also included in the music series books.

Characteristics of the Kodály Program

1. Kodály saw as the purpose of music education the creation of a musically literate population. "Is it imaginable that anybody who is unable to read words can acquire a literary culture or knowledge of any kind? Equally, no musical knowledge of any kind can be acquired without the reading of music" (Kodály, 1969, p. 10). This interest in understanding notation is in contrast to Orff and Jaques-Dalcroze, and it led Kodály to several techniques for teaching children to be literate musicians.

Before developing the Music Primary School program, Kodály made an intensive study of the existing systems of teaching music in many countries. From England he adopted two techniques. One was a system of hand signs developed about a century earlier by John Curwen. The other, which is closely related to the hand signs, is the use of the *sol-fa,* or movable *do,* pitch syllables. In movable *do* the tonic note in major is always *do.* Therefore, the syllables represent relative pitch relationships, not fixed pitches as they do in solfège. The hand positions, which are a form of kinesthetic reinforcement of the relative pitch, were altered slightly by Kodály. They are shown in Figure 9.3. Kodály also adopted Curwen's idea of abbreviating the syllable names to only the first letter. These letters are not intended to replace standard pitch names; their purpose is to aid in learning pitch relationships.

The pitch syllables are presented in an order similar to that used in Orff's *Schulwerk: sol, mi, la, do, re,* and then later in second grade (third grade in the nonmusic primary schools) *fa* and *ti.* In later years *fi, si,* and *ta* are added, and music that modulates is sung with these syllables. During the primary years of instruction, much of the music sung is pentatonic. Kodály found that children tend to sing the fourth slightly sharp and the seventh slightly flat, and that the pentatonic scale eliminates these problems. Also, the pentatonic scale is strongly rooted in Hungarian folk music.

2. The learning of patterns and motives is an important aspect of the Kodály approach. For the most part, they are derived from the music the students are singing. The more common patterns are practiced persistently, and the students are made aware of them. In this way the students' sense of syntax for music is aided.

3. Rhythm patterns are also taught by relating them to the material being sung. Rhythmic values are represented visually by a vertical line or stem for a quarter note and by a pair of vertical lines joined together at the top by a brace or ligature for an eighth note, as in the example on page 127.

$$\frac{2}{4} \; | \; | \; | \; \sqcap \; | \; |$$

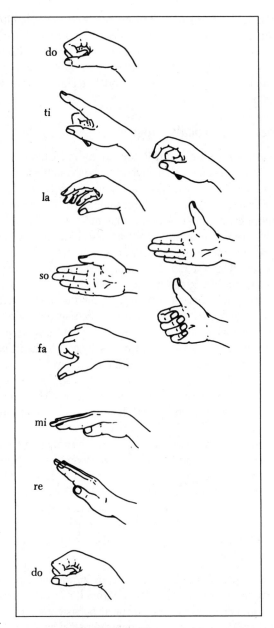

Figure 9.3   *Curwen-Kodály hand signs.*

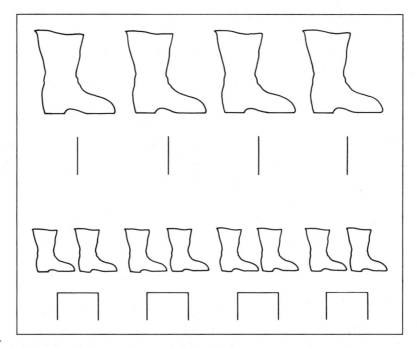

Figure 9.5 *Pictorial presentation of notes and their lengths.*

Rhythmic syllables are often said to the note values: "ta" for a quarter note and "ti" (pronounced "tee") for each eighth. Half notes are said "Ta-a," dotted half notes "ta-a-a," and whole notes "ta-a-a-a."

Initially the notes are presented pictorially with the size of the notes adjusted to give the children an indication of the length of the note. (See Figure 9.5.)

4. Music in the Kodály program is largely taught through singing. Kodály was a strong believer in using the voice: "Only the human voice, which is a possession of everyone, and at the same time the most beautiful of all instruments, can serve as the basis for a general music culture" (Kraus, 1990, p. 81). Recorder playing is introduced in second or third grade after a solid foundation has been laid through singing. Little enthusiasm is expressed for the piano. Since Hungary is not a wealthy country, there aren't many pianos in the schools anyway.

5. One of the reasons Kodály so strongly favored unaccompanied singing was his wish to have children develop an accurate sense of pitch and the ability to hear music in their minds. Hungarian school students do sing in a far more polished manner than their American counterparts. Their intonation seems impeccable and their vocal timbre pure.

Many activities are designed to develop inner hearing. In addition to listening carefully to intonation in both unison and part singing, the students sing music silently in their minds. A song is sung aloud until the teacher signals silence, at which time the students continue it in their minds. Singing aloud is resumed upon another signal from the teacher. Sometimes the students read a short song silently. After they have memorized it, the music is covered up or erased, and they sing it aloud.

6. Kodály was firmly convinced that music instruction should start at an early age, well before the children enter elementary school.

> Obviously, all reasonable pedagogy has to start from the first spontaneous utterances of the child, rhythmic-melodic expressions with repeated simple phrases which slowly give way to more complex structures. Since children learn most easily between the ages of three and six, the kindergartens would be able to accomplish much more in music if they would observe this pedagogic principle (Kodály, 1990, p. 75).

This belief in the importance of the initial efforts in learning music is the opposite of that of many American music teachers, who devote much of their attention to the performing groups in the secondary schools. Kodály points out that without a solid foundation in the early years, the results later on will be stunted.

7. The music used for the first several years of the curriculum consists largely of Hungarian folk songs. The association of the Kodály method with its folk and nationalistic roots is something that is often overlooked by foreigners. Hungary is a rather small nation with a population about the size of Ohio. Several times in its past it has experienced long occupations by outsiders—Turks, Austrians, Germans, and Russians. Two things make it possible for Hungarians to retain their national identity under such circumstances: their language (which is most closely related to Finnish) and their music. Therefore, a knowledge of music is especially significant to Hungarians. It is impossible to know how much this feeling of nationalism influenced Kodály when he developed the program following World War II. In one sense it doesn't matter, because his ideas clearly have proved that they have validity without any nationalistic associations.

His views on the value of folk music are clear.

> I dare say we may attribute this [successful] result mostly to the folk song, which is our chief material. Folk songs offer such a rich variety of moods and perspective, that the child grows in human consciousness and feels more and more at home in his country. . . .
>
> To become international we first have to belong to one distinct people and to speak its language properly, not in gibberish. To understand other people, we must first understand ourselves. And nothing will accomplish this better than a thorough knowledge of one's native folk songs (Kodály, 1969, p. 143).

8. The Kodály program strongly emphasizes music of a high quality. No commercial popular music is found in the program. "In art," Kodály has written, "bad taste is a real spiritual illness. It is the duty of the school to offer protection against this plague. . . . The goal is: To educate children in such a way that they find music indispensable to life . . . of course good artistic music" (Kraus, 1990, p. 84).

SUZUKI TALENT EDUCATION

Development and Background

With the work of Shinichi Suzuki (b. 1898), this chapter shifts from vocal-general music to instrumental music. Suzuki's views on teaching the violin are heavily laced with the belief that musical talent is a product of one's upbringing. "All human beings are born with great potentialities," Suzuki has said, "and each individual has within himself, the capacity for developing to a very high level" (Kendall, 1966, p. 9). The belief in the universal nature of music talent led to the inclusion of "Talent Education" in the name of the program.

Suzuki's father owned a violin factory, and he learned about violins and how to play them as a boy. His study also included eight years in Berlin in the 1920s. Before World War II he formed a string quartet of himself and three brothers and did some teaching. After the war he started teaching young people to play the violin. His accomplishments as a teacher first became known in the United States in 1958 at a meeting of the American String Teachers Association at Oberlin College, when a film of 750 Japanese children playing Bach's Concerto for Two Violins was shown. A year later John Kendall traveled to Japan to observe Suzuki at work, and he made a second trip in 1962. In 1964, the American String Teachers Association presented Suzuki and ten of his students, who ranged in age from ten to fourteen, at the MENC national convention in Philadelphia. The impact on the audience was electric. Few of the teachers in the audience had ever heard young students play so musically and so well. Following that appearance, hundreds of workshops on the method have been held, and Suzuki has made several more trips to the United States with his students. For several reasons that will become apparent shortly, the impact of the Suzuki approach in the public schools has been somewhat limited, but his ideas have certainly been influential.

Characteristics of Suzuki Talent Education

1. Suzuki strongly favors beginning instruction at an early age; in fact, the younger, the better. Violin instruction in the Talent Education program usually begins at three years of age, but it can begin earlier. He favors playing good recordings for children while they are still in the crib, and, for several weeks before the first lesson, the parents every day play the recordings of the violin pieces the child will study later. Then the child attends a few lessons and watches and listens to what is going on; this is followed by being given an instrument.

It should be pointed out that string instruments, unlike many other instruments, can be adjusted in size, which facilitates working with young children. Many of Suzuki's youngest pupils begin on a 1/16th-sized violin. As they grow larger, they are given larger instruments until they play a full-sized violin.

2. The method of learning is rote imitation. The student hears something and attempts to imitate it. Suzuki believes that music is learned in much the same way that language is learned. He has pointed out, "All children in the world show their splendid capacities by speaking and understanding their mother language, thus displaying the original power of the human mind" (Kendall, 1966, p. 9).

The imitating of an aural model is an aspect of Suzuki's pedagogy that seems to be often overlooked. Not only does it help the students to play musically and without the mechanical qualities often associated with beginning instrument study, it appears to guide students over technical problems, even those for which they have had no specific instruction.

3. All the music the student performs is memorized. The technical matters of playing music on the instrument are learned first, and then the student may begin looking at notation. Of course, reading by three-year-old children is out of the question because their eye muscles have not developed sufficiently to allow them to focus on objects the size of music and printed material. The parents use the books and follow the music to help the children practice, however.

When reading is introduced after some years of study, the process is one of following the notation of a work that the student already knows. In this way, the logic of music notation is more easily understood because it is a process of visualizing what has already been learned.

4. Whatever is learned by the students is learned thoroughly. For example, while the students are playing a work such as the Vivaldi Concerto in A Minor, the teacher may direct them to do knee bends or walk up and down stairs. Sometimes a group of students is divided in half. One half plays while the other half follows along silently, ready to pick up the music on a moment's notice without causing a break in the flow. The entire work is performed alternating between the two groups with no interruptions.

5. One of the parents, usually the mother, attends the lessons and learns the violin along with the child. Suzuki wants the parents involved in order to impress the child with the importance of the activity, and also so that they can help in guiding the home practicing.

6. The lessons are private and rather short, especially for the younger students. If a child yawns, the lesson is concluded. The students and teacher stand throughout the lesson. This helps maintain a better position and also contributes to better attention. The room is kept free from distractions because Suzuki wants the student to concentrate on playing the violin. Often other children observe a lesson and perhaps join in the playing of one number.

7. All students, regardless of ability, learn the same sequence of music. Some students may go through it faster than others, but all study the same works in the same order. Therefore, all Suzuki students have the same repertoire, which makes it easy to combine them for large group performances without prior rehearsals. The materials almost completely lack etudes and scales, which used to be dear to the hearts of many instrumental music teachers. Instead, shifting, vibrato, bowing, and so on are dealt with in relation to their appearance in works of music; technical exercises are drawn from the setting in the music. Suzuki avoids what he terms "manufactured material" before advanced levels are achieved.

8. The ten manuals or books contain carefully selected music, much of it by Bach, Handel, and Vivaldi. Recordings are available for the works in the first five or six volumes, and recordings made by artist violinists are used for the other works, which are standard concert pieces.

9. Cooperation, not competition, is fostered among the students. Students of all levels of advancement play together, and older students help the younger students. An attitude of mutual respect is maintained among parents, teachers, and students.

Suzuki-like instruction is available from private teachers in a number of communities in the United States. Also, adaptations of Suzuki's ideas for teaching the violin have been made, with his approval and at his school in Japan, for the cello and the piano. The only concession to size on the piano is the use of a box to raise the height of the pedals for the small children. America is not Japan, of course, and a number of cultural factors make some of Suzuki's ideas more difficult to carry out here. Nevertheless, some students who have started in Suzuki-like programs in this country have succeeded very well.

FOREIGN METHODS IN AMERICAN SCHOOLS

Music teachers who are professional about their work are constantly examining and considering new teaching ideas. One source of fresh ideas is the successful methods from other countries. However, as successful as many of these methods are in their native land, American music educators should keep several facts in mind about adopting or adapting them.

It is not possible to pick up an educational program from Hungary or Japan or any other country (except maybe Canada) and drop it down intact in the United States. Why? Because there are significant musical, educational, and cultural differences between each country and the United States. A musical difference, for example, can be found in the use of 6/8 meter. Many children's songs in America ("Pop Goes the Weasel," "When Johnny Comes Marching Home," and others) are in 6/8, but it is not so common in Hungary. In that country the introduction of 6/8 meter is held off until the fourth grade level, which would not be sensible in America. On the other hand, the pentatonic scale is found frequently in Hungarian folk music but is somewhat rare in American folk music. If the music program is to be based on folk music, as Kodály strongly suggests, then in America much less use will have to be made of the pentatonic scale.

There are also important educational differences among the countries of the world. For example, schools in most European countries have a shorter school day than American schools but do not offer extracurricular activities or provide lunches. The one or two hours that this makes available to European school students can be used in a variety of ways, one of which is music study at a community music school. Therefore, much less music, especially instrumental music, is taught during the school day in most European schools. In some countries the secondary schools are either academic or trade schools; the comprehensive high school that is the ideal in the United States does not exist in most countries (and in many places in the United States, but that is another topic). The nature of these schools, then, differs from that of most American secondary schools.

American music educators also need to keep in mind that *Schulwerk* and Suzuki violin instruction are almost never taught in the public schools of the countries with which they are associated. They were designed for and are taught in private schools that charge the students a tuition. Dalcroze eurhythmics are taught in some public school systems in Swiss cities, but seldom in the schools of other countries. Even the Kodály program is basically for a special type of school that is very different from the average American elementary school.

There are also cultural differences among nations, some of which are subtle and difficult to describe in a few sentences. For example, while observing Suzuki's work in Japan, John Kendall talked with a sixteen-year-old boy about studying violin. Although he planned to become an engineer someday, the young man was faithfully practicing his violin a couple of hours each day. The high school he attended did not have an orchestra for him to play in, and community orchestras are rare in Japan, so Kendall realized that the boy had no place to play the violin with others, and probably would not in the future. Why then, Kendall asked, was he working so diligently at the violin? "Because it is good for my soul," was the young man's response (J. Kendall, personal communication, April 1965). It is indeed difficult to imagine a similar response from a sixteen-year-old American student!

Although it may be difficult to transplant a music teaching approach that works well in Germany or Japan to the United States, it is quite easy to adopt some techniques from a method. Kodály himself adopted the hand signs from the Englishman Curwen, and they can rather easily be adopted by American music teachers. The same is true of some techniques from each of the methods described in this chapter. However, there is much more to each of these methods than their techniques. Jaques-Dalcroze, Orff, Kodály, and Suzuki each have more to offer the world than a few teaching "recipes," gimmicks, or teaching procedures. Just having students put on leotards and move to music does not mean that one is teaching eurhythmics, any more than playing an ostinato or a metallophone means that one is following the Orff method. Although the methods contain the features listed in this chapter, there is much more to them than those features.

American music educators need to be careful when adapting any approach from another country. Such adaptations should be undertaken only after a thorough knowledge of the particular method has been acquired. Thomas Huxley was correct when he wrote, "A little knowledge is dangerous" (Huxley, 1968, p. 725). A misuse of a teaching method may do more harm than good, to say nothing of being a distortion of the original.

Questions

1. In what ways are the methods of Émile Jaques-Dalcroze and Carl Orff similar?

2. In what ways are the methods of Carl Orff and Zoltán Kodály different?

3. What are the differences between solfège (fixed *do*) and movable *do*?

4. Why does the Orff-*Schulwerk* program begin with speech patterns?

5. In what ways do Hungarian Music Primary Schools differ from most elementary schools in America?

6. How do hand signs or other hand movements help students to sing on pitch more accurately?

7. Why did Kodály favor singing instead of playing instruments in the early grades?

8. In what way is Suzuki's method of learning to play the violin similar to the way children learn to speak?

9. Why is it necessary for American music teachers to adapt methods developed in other countries?

Project
Interview an elementary music specialist about the contributions of Dalcroze, Orff, or Kodály. Specifically ask about the benefits of the particular approach for American students and the points in the particular methods that need to be adapted for use in American schools.

References
Becknell, A. F. (1970). *A history of the development of Dalcroze eurhythmics in the United States and its influence on the public school music program*. Doctoral dissertation, University of Michigan.

Carder, P. (Ed.). (1990). *The eclectic curriculum in American music education: Contributions of Dalcroze, Kodály, and Orff* (2nd ed.). Reston, VA: Music Educators National Conference.

Dobbs, J. (1968, August). Some great music educators: Emile Jaques-Dalcroze. *Music teacher, 47*(8), p. 13.

Hoffer, C. R. (1981). How widely are Kodály and Orff approaches used? *Music Educators Journal, 67*(6), 46–47.

Huxley, T. H. (1968). On Elemental Instruction Physiology. Quoted in J. Bartlett, *Bartlett's Familiar Quotations* (14th ed.) (p. 725). (E. M. Beck, Ed.). Boston: Little, Brown.

Kendall, J. (1966). *Talent education and Suzuki*. Reston, VA: Music Educators National Conference.

Kodály, Z. (1969). *Visszatekintes*. In H. Szabo, *The Kodály concept of music education*. (G. Russell-Smith, Trans.). London: Boosey and Hawkes. (Original work published 1964)

Kraus, E. (1990). Zoltán Kodály's legacy to music education. In P. Carder (Ed.), *The eclectic curriculum in American music education: Contributions of Dalcroze, Kodály, and Orff* (2nd ed.) (pp. 79–92). Reston, VA: Music Educators National Conference.

Orff, C. (1990). The *Schulwerk*—its origins and aims. (A. Walter, Trans.). In P. Carder (Ed.), *The eclectic curriculum in American music education: Contributions of Dalcroze, Kodály, and Orff* (2nd ed.) (pp. 137–144). Reston, VA: Music Educators National Conference.

Pennington, J. (1925). *The importance of being rhythmic: A study of the principles of Dalcroze eurhythmics applied to general education and to the arts of music dancing, and acting*. Based on and adapted from *Rhythm, music and education* by E. Jaques-Dalcroze. New York: G. P. Putnam's Sons.

CHAPTER 10

Challenges in Music Education

*C*harles Dickens began his *Tale of Two Cities* with these memorable words: "It was the best of times; it was the worst of times." While that sentiment is a bit strong when talking about the current condition of music education, it does contain an important idea for future music teachers to keep in mind. Yes, there are problems now, and there will be problems in the future. However, the "flip side" of a problem is an opportunity, a chance to take corrective actions. It is through taking such actions that music education advances.

This chapter discusses a number of the problems/opportunities that music educators will need to deal with now and in the near future. To the extent that they are successful in dealing with them, music education will continue to grow and improve. In a real sense, the future will largely be determined by those who teach music in schools now and will do so in the future.

MUSIC IN EARLY CHILDHOOD

During the past ten or fifteen years the percentage of three-, four- and five-year-old children enrolled in some type of school has grown tremendously. It is now estimated that 50 percent of all four-year-olds are receiving some form of school-

ing. Ninety percent of all five-year-olds are in kindergarten (Andress, 1989). These schools and the children they serve represent a major opportunity for music education.

Research evidence points to the importance of learning during these early years. There are musical skills (matching pitch, for example) that children learn best when they are young; they don't learn them as well later. Although teaching a child to sense the beat or sing a simple song may not appear to be a high-level musical or intellectual activity, it is extremely important in terms of the child's musical development later on. Not only is the particular musical skill involved, the child's attitude toward music is also affected. Children who do not do as well as their classmates in music usually realize it, and that fact often gives them a negative attitude toward their participation in music and toward music in general. The approaches of Dalcroze, Orff, Kodály, and Suzuki discussed in Chapter 9 all emphasize the importance of teaching children music at an early age. For some reason, until recently few American music educators were concerned about what children learned in the years before and during kindergarten.

Music instruction is very important for three-, four-, and five-year-olds, and it is in need of much attention. Few school systems operate programs for children before kindergarten. State laws on education generally mention starting school at age 5 or 6, and seldom does any state financially support educating children younger than that. The few regulations that exist usually cite physical plant specifications and adult/child ratios, but say nothing about the curriculum. Most preschools are operated by churches, corporations, Head Start, or individuals. Usually the workers, often called "care givers," are not certified teachers. Many of them are hired at the minimum hourly wage and have a limited education themselves. As the name care giver implies, preschools are often seen as providing child care; educational benefits are secondary in many of them. The music the children usually receive, then, too often consists of singing along with or engaging in physical actions to recordings. Some schools don't even do that.

Because so many preschool students are missing out on gaining musical skills, and because the learning of such skills is vital at an early age, MENC has made music in early childhood a priority for special attention. A task force was formed to develop actions. Among other things, it developed a policy statement on music for preschool children and kindergartners that was adopted by the National Executive Board in 1991. In part, it reads as follows:

> Music is a natural and important part of young children's growth and development. Early interaction with music positively affects the quality of all children's lives. Successful experiences in music help all children bond emotionally and intellectually with others through creative expression in song, rhythmic movement, and listening experiences. Music in early childhood creates a foundation upon which future music learning is built. These experiences should be integrated within the daily routine and play of children. In this way, enduring attitudes regarding the joy of music making and sharing are developed.
>
> Music education for young children involves a developmentally appropriate program of singing, moving, listening, creating, playing instruments, and responding to visual and verbal representations of sound. The content of such a program should represent music of various cultures in time and place. Time should be made available during the day for activities in which music is the primary focus of attention for its own value. It may also serve as a means for teachers to facilitate the accomplishment of nonmusical goals.
>
> Musical experiences should be play-based and planned for various types of learning opportunities such as one-on-one, choice time, integration with other areas of the curriculum, and large group music focus. The best possible musical models and activities should be provided. Adults responsible for guiding these experiences may range from parent, to care giver, to early childhood educator, to music specialist. Music educators are committed to working in partnership with these adults to provide exemplary music experiences for young children. (*Soundpost,* p. 21)

The position statement also lists ten beliefs about music for young children:

1. All children have musical potential.
2. Children bring their own unique interests and abilities to the music learning environment.
3. Very young children are capable of developing critical thinking skills through musical ideas.

4. Children come to early childhood music experiences from diverse backgrounds.

5. Children should experience exemplary musical sounds, activities, and materials.

6. Children should not be encumbered with the need to meet performance goals.

7. Children's play is their work.

8. Children learn best in pleasant physical and social environments.

9. Diverse learning environments are needed to serve the developmental needs of many individual children.

10. Children need effective adult models.

To someone who plans to teach choral or instrumental music at the high school level, the music education of young children may not seem all that important. Wrong. Although the results of good music instruction may not show up for ten or more years, it will show up sometime in improved musical skills and attitudes. The general level of musical interest and proficiency will have been raised. When that happens, everyone benefits.

MUSIC IN MIDDLE SCHOOLS

The problem of music for students in grades 6, 7, 8, and even 9 is a perennial one. The students in these grades are in a state of rapid transition from child to adult status. These grade levels contain a mixture of maturity and immaturity, which in itself is an interesting challenge and opportunity.

Educators over the years have had a hard time deciding what type of education is best for students at this age. For many years, elementary schools went through grade 8; high school began with grade 9. There was no transition. Then came the junior high school, which was a junior version of high school, with students moving from teacher to teacher for different subjects. However, including ninth grade presented real difficulties. Its courses had to meet certain criteria for inclusion on transcripts for college entrance, and ninth graders are generally much more mature than seventh graders.

The answer to these difficulties seemed to be the middle school, which was intended to be a real transition between elementary and high school. However, middle schools also present some dilemmas. Some include grades 5 through 8, some 6 through 8, and other combinations are also called middle schools. Disagreement exists over the nature of the middle school curriculum. Some educators want middle schools to include "exploratory" experiences in certain areas (but not in "basics" such as mathematics and English). Usually music is included in the exploratory package, or "wheel," of courses six to nine weeks in length. The exploratory idea would be more acceptable if there were room in the school day for it, say seven or even eight periods plus lunch. Unfortunately, many times the exploratory courses are jammed into a six-period day, which must be something like getting a size 10 foot into a size 7 shoe. Other music courses suffer when such curriculum squeezing is attempted.

Music teachers do not agree either on what music in the middle schools should be like. Sometimes the teaching, especially in performing groups, is very much like what is found in most high schools. And in truth, some of the directors of performing organizations in middle schools hope to move on to bigger and better things by landing a high school job as soon as possible. In other cases, general music classes are taught in a manner similar to what is provided to students in grades 4 and 5.

The sad part about all this is that many middle school students are not receiving the kind of music education they should. One exploratory experience in grade 6 or 7, lasting for six or nine weeks, can hardly be considered an adequate education in music. *The School Music Program: Description and Standards* recommends ninety class periods each year in grades 6 and 7 plus reasonable elective experiences in all grades (MENC, 1986). The same MENC publication states that members of performing groups should also take general music and that performing groups should meet daily.

The saddest point of all about inadequate middle school programs is that they are the culminating music instruction for many students. Think of it, the majority of the students do not take music in high school, which means that their music instruction concludes when they are eleven or twelve years old. Is it any wonder, then, that a majority of people in America exhibit what might be termed a "twelve-year-old's" understanding of music?

In 1990 MENC identified music in middle schools as a priority area of concern. Indeed, it is a topic of vital importance to music educators. If what was is past is prologue, then it will be around for many years to come.

ASSESSMENT OF LEARNING

A criticism of American schools heard often in recent years concerns the lack of standards for learning by the students. Students complete courses and grade levels, but what did they have to know and be able to do to pass those courses and grades? Occasionally real "horror stories" appear in the newspapers about students who finish high school and yet are functionally illiterate. The reasons such persons are allowed to graduate are complex and beyond the scope of this discussion. Whatever they are, such instances cannot be justified, and they offer a depressing comment on American education.

One remedy to the problem of standards heard frequently is the assessment of student learning in various academic areas at two or three different grade levels. This idea has two problems: (1) There is little agreement about exactly what it is the students should be learning at various levels of a subject, and (2) there is little agreement about how learning can or should be assessed. The unfortunate fact is that the aspects of a subject most easily tested are usually the less important ones. For example, it is easy to tell if a person knows the names of the notes on the grand staff. But how important is that knowledge in the subject of music? Is it as important as the concept of development in symphonic music or as the idea of modulation?

Music faces some special problems in coming up with measurable criteria for assessment. First, it cannot be tested adequately through paper-and-pencil tests. Music educators want students to be able to sing a song reasonably well, not only be able to define what a song is. They want students to hear features of music, not only recognize the title and composer of a work.

Music teachers could refuse to assess student learning. However, if the assessment of learning is done in other subjects, music has little choice but to go along. You can't claim music is an area equal to others in importance and then be unwilling or unable to assess learning in it. At least you can't do that and be consistent and logical. Therefore, making the assessment of learning in music as valid and precise as possible is a challenge and an opportunity for music educators. It is an opportunity for music teachers to become much clearer and more adept at determining how well students have learned. Too often teachers have assumed that students are learning whatever is being taught, when in fact very little learning is taking place.

Another challenge is not letting tests determine what is to be taught. Assessment is supposed to measure how well the students have learned what they were to learn. However, it is easy for teachers to reverse that process and to begin to select the content of classes based on what they think will appear on a test. Teachers need to remember which is more important, learning or testing.

EDUCATION VERSUS ENTERTAINMENT

Music is fun; it is enjoyable. This can be both a blessing and a curse. It is a blessing because people enjoy making and listening to music. It can be a curse when the entertainment value of music distracts students, teachers, and the community from the educational reasons for having music in the schools in the first place.

The education/entertainment dilemma affects very few areas of the school curriculum. No one thinks of learning about compounds in chemistry or practicing pronunciations in Spanish class as entertaining; no one sells tickets to a chemistry concert or a Spanish-language proficiency recital. The only other curricular area comparable to music in entertainment possibilities is physical education with its competitive games.

The similarities between music and physical education are interesting. Both areas have general programs for all students. Both areas have specialists (coaches and directors) who are hardly involved with the general program. Both areas have performing groups (marching bands or musicals and competitive games) that receive most of the attention but involve only a small percentage of the students.

There is another important way in which coaches of athletic teams and directors of performing groups are similar: They both present groups publicly, something teachers in other areas almost never do. The performance of music for the public often exerts strong feelings of pressure on teachers, many of which are self-imposed. The tendency for teachers is to do whatever it takes to present a performance that the audience will applaud. Therefore, actions are taken to make the group perform as well as possible: learn fewer works but perform those works well; select music that will draw a positive response from the audience; restrict membership in the group to those students less likely to make errors and generally more capable; and consider performance to be the main purpose of the group. It takes a strong person to resist the temptation to slip over the line from teaching students to being a producer of entertainment. As someone has pointed out, "The applause of an audience is pretty heady wine." Once tasted, it becomes nearly addictive for some music teachers.

There are some differences between athletic teams and musical organizations. The music groups earn grades and credits and meet during the school day because they are considered educational. The word *educational* is the key to the difference here. The education of the athletic team members is limited only to learning how to play the particular game better. In contrast, music groups such as the band, orchestra, and choir should be the means by which students learn music better.

As if pressures resulting from public performances weren't enough, music teachers teach an elective subject. They have to make their courses attractive so that enough students enroll in them to fill a teaching schedule. In addition, in times of tight budgets, school administrators and school boards tend to reduce funds for elective subjects more than they do subjects considered "basic." In view of all these factors, it is not surprising that music teachers too often surrender to entertainment and the pleasing of audiences.

Part of the solution to handling the entertainment/education dilemma lies in reducing the pressures that music teachers feel to appeal to audiences. Personal integrity is fine, but why make things more difficult than they need to be? Some of the pressure can be reduced by educating students, other teachers, school administrators and board members, and the community about the value and the purposes of music in the schools. But more on this important matter shortly.

Some deeper issues regarding entertainment and education lie beyond the scope of this discussion. Basically those issues involve what is implied by the concepts of entertainment and of education and how the two concepts relate to each other.

INFORMING OTHERS ABOUT MUSIC EDUCATION

Music teachers must understand and believe in what they are teaching. And as important as that is, it's not enough. Unfortunately, music teachers do not determine how much money they will be allocated in the school budget, the number of staff members in their subject matter area, if a music room will be included in a new elementary school, if music and the fine arts are included in the graduation requirements from high school, and on and on. Such decisions are made by others, usually school administrators, school board members, and state legislators. Therefore, music educators need to educate these decision makers about what is needed to support a good music program and why it is needed. Unless music teachers engage in educating others about their school music program, there is a real chance that someday their program will be questioned, especially in years when budgets are tight.

Some of this task must be assumed by each music teacher. MENC and its state units can help raise the consciousness of people regarding the importance of music, and they can offer support. But in each school in each school district it is the music teacher who must educate his or her principal and parents. Unless informed about the nature and the purposes of the school music program, very few administrators will know what that program should be and what it is trying to accomplish. Their backgrounds are usually in other fields, often physical education, and in no place during their professional preparation do they learn in any depth about music education.

Informing others about music education may sound like a lot of work, but it need not be. It doesn't take hours of extra time. One hour a week on average is usually all that is needed for such activities.

If persons not in music need to be informed about music in the schools, what "message" should they be given? What should they be told? First, the message must be more than a slogan. "Support school music" is a nice thought, but it says nothing about why school music should be supported or what one can do to support it. Basically, the message should meet two criteria.

1. It must be understandable to people who are not musicians. Polysyllabic, vague verbiage won't work.
2. The message must be accurate and true. Exaggerated claims about music building teamwork or citizenship won't stand up under thoughtful scrutiny. Besides, if improved citizenship or health is a goal of a school, the logical places to turn to are social science or health-physical education courses, not music.

The importance of music for all students can be explained from two different viewpoints. One is through objective data about the importance of music throughout all civilizations and its importance in contemporary America. It is easy to assemble data about the sums of money spent on recordings and concerts, the number of Americans who play instruments or sing in choral groups, and so on. And these figures are pretty impressive.

The other viewpoint involves subjective feelings. Most people sense—correctly—that music is a worthwhile activity, and they feel good when they hear young people singing in a choral group or playing their instruments. Even if they can't express in words why they feel this way, they do. These subjective but positive feelings are something that music education has going for it.

The objective and subjective approaches should both be used to gain support for music education. Information about the importance of music should be made available. In addition, people need to hear the students in performances, and especially in "informances." The factual material and observations of students making and learning music show that it is valuable for everyone. The two approaches make the point that no one should miss the chance to learn about music; no young person should be denied this opportunity for a richer life. The main point to make is this: *Young people should not be cheated out of the chance to learn music.* Just as no one wants students to graduate from high school incompetent in the use of the English language and uninformed about science, no one should want them to complete school ignorant about music.

What are some things music teachers can do to inform others about music in the schools? Here is a short list from among the many things that can be done:

1. Prepare a written report to the principal or superintendent, even if one is not requested. A thoughtful, articulate discussion of the music program and its needs will make a positive impression, even if no action can be taken at that moment. At least one such report each year is suggested.

2. Make school performances into "informances" in which the audience learns about both music and what the students are learning in music.

3. Send information about the school music program to local newspapers, the school district newsletter, a cable television outlet (which is required to have a local access channel), and other media. Such items need to be "newsy"; they can include information about special music, student accomplishments, and the like.

4. Seek out chances to perform for civic groups like the Rotary club. During the performance mention facts such as the names of students who participated in special music events over the summer or are involved in music in college. In addition, explain something about the music being performed and what the students are learning from singing or playing it.

5. Strongly encourage the band boosters and other parent organizations to support the entire music program by making their views be known to school administrators and board members. By working for improvements in the middle school general music program, for example, the boosters can help the music education program without spending more than a few dollars for mailings and telephone calls.

6. Work with private music teachers, professional musicians, music merchants, and others in the community who already have positive feelings about music and who sometimes have a financial interest in the musical health of the community.

7. Join with other music educators at the state level to develop contacts with departments of education, legislators, and other decision makers.

Maybe it's unfair that science and social science teachers don't have to educate people about the value of their subjects, but music teachers do. Fair or not, it is a simple fact of life for music educators. It "comes with the territory," as the saying goes. Music teachers cannot afford to neglect this portion of their "territory."

FUND-RAISING

Fund-raising for school music groups is a two-edged sword. One edge is that fund-raising benefits many school music organizations. It really has helped purchase needed material and equipment. In other cases, the extra funds allowed for enrichment activities that pumped life into the music organization.

The negative edge of the sword, however, is that fund-raising cuts deeply into the well-being of music in the schools. How? In four basic areas: (1) time and effort, (2) balance in the music program, (3) public image, and (4) the curricular status of music.

The first area, time and effort, is a concern because in too many situations fund-raising uses class or rehearsal time, and time is almost always in short supply for music instruction. In addition, time and effort are required on the part of both students and parents to raise the funds. The music teachers involved must commit their energies to such activities. Because there are only so many hours in the day, these efforts almost certainly take away from some of the time that the teachers could have spent on planning for or teaching students.

Fund-raising efforts are usually only for specific performing organizations, not the overall music program, the second way in which fund-raising injures school music programs. The groups for which funds are raised are given much visibility, while the other portions of the program (the ones involving the vast majority of the students) go largely unnoticed. Seldom does one hear about a fund-raising effort for fifth grade general music classes! The result is a major imbalance in many music programs in which one or two performing groups become *the* music program in the eyes of most people, while the classes for most of the students are ignored.

In many communities the group for which funds are raised is thought to be the measure of success for the entire music program. For example, the fact that one group raised money for a trip (from which they secured some favorable local press coverage) is seen as proof that the school district has a fine music program. Sometimes that assumption is accurate, but generally it is not. The quality of any one performing group in a school district usually tells little about the remainder of the program.

Fund-raising also carries with it some heavy baggage in terms of the image it presents, the third way music education suffers from such activities. When most of the public's contact with school music is with fund-raising activities for trips to some attractive place, it is difficult to avoid forming a mental association between music and extracurricular activities. After all, students do not hold car washes or sell candy for science or English classes! Fund-raising encourages the view of music as a frill, something nice but not all that important. Fund-raising tends to undercut the efforts to promote music as a worthy subject for study. When most of what people see of the school music program is its glitz and tinsel, it should not be surprising when they fail to support it in times of restricted budgets.

There is yet another way in which fund-raising hurts school music programs. Once a music group establishes a record of success in securing funding, the school administrators then tend to let music take care of itself financially. The money saved on music, the administrators logically conclude, can always be used for other worthwhile needs in the school. Because of fund-raising activities, some directors of performing groups have virtually taken their music organizations out of the school budget, whether they intended to do so or not.

Unfortunately, the benefits of fund-raising are no match for the damage that has been done to music programs in many school districts and to music education generally. The two edges of the sword do not have equal impact.

To begin the process of correcting the situations, a MENC task force was appointed in 1989. It developed a policy statement, which was reviewed by MENC state and division boards and revised by the National Executive Board before adoption in 1990. The full text of the policy appears in Appendix C.

The basic ideas of the policy are simple. First, the curricular program of music instruction should be funded entirely from the school budget. Second, there may be some enrichment activities for students in music classes that cannot normally be supported from the school budget. Third, fund-raising for these enrichment activities should be kept within reasonable limits, including avoiding the use of class or rehearsal time and large-scale projects that involve hundreds of hours and many thousands of dollars. Fourth, the success of the first three points in the policy statement depends on the willingness and ability of music teachers to provide guidance in fund-raising efforts. Fifth, fund-raising efforts should not put youngsters at risk. Implementing this policy is a challenge and an opportunity for MENC and for all music educators.

CULTURAL DIVERSITY

There are compelling reasons for music educators to teach some types of music in addition to traditional Western art and folk music. Everyday the world seems drawn more closely together. Television presents stories from around the world, and millions of people visit each other's countries each year. The world is truly a "global village." Furthermore, students from a wide variety of cultures live in America and attend school, and that proportion of the school population grows larger each year. No longer is it likely that a young person can grow up having no exposure to at least a few persons from another country and culture.

The fact that there are good reasons for including a variety of types of music in school curricula does not mean it is an easy thing to do well. First, there is the matter of time for instruction. If an elementary music teacher has only thirty or forty minutes a week with a class, one doesn't need to think too hard about it to realize that this is not much time. Adding more types of music presents real problems in such a situation.

Second, no music teacher can teach many different types of music well. Each type possesses subtleties that require extensive training to understand or to perform authentically. If music teachers have trouble knowing many different types of music, what about the students who don't know any kind of music very well? This fact raises a dilemma: How far from the original character of the music can a performance stray before it becomes a travesty instead of a useful educational experience? There are no clear answers, of course, but it is a matter that each music teacher must think about.

Third, music is very much intertwined with the culture in which it exists. This fact is both beneficial and detrimental. The good news is that music has a valuable role in helping students learn about the world's peoples. The negative side is that the close relationship with culture means that the job of teaching a variety of kinds of music is complex. It includes not only the musical sounds but also the cultural and social setting of the music.

Fourth, the number of kinds of music around the world is huge. At best, a music teacher can cover only a tiny portion of them.

Although it is not easy, music teachers need to expand the types of music covered from what has been traditionally taught. These suggestions can help in doing this:

1. Make a careful selection of music from the types found around the world, one that is as representative as possible.

2. Make sure that the works selected are good examples for the particular types of music. Then, spend enough class time on those works so that they are really learned by the students. Skimming over many works is not effective for most students.

3. Present the music of non-Western cultures as authentically as possible. Usually this involves the use of recordings, although sometimes a competent performer of a particular type of music lives in the community. Student performances should be attempted *after* they have heard an authentic performance.

4. Most important of all, attempt to instill in the students an attitude of respect and acceptance toward all kinds of music. The attitudes that students acquire about different kinds of music are much more important than what they learn in terms of information.

The need for a more diverse music curriculum presents music educators with an opportunity to develop music programs that are more interesting. At the same time they will be making them more representative of the pluralistic nature of American society.

STUDENTS AT RISK

At one time, schools were thought to be centers for academic activity that were somehow insulated from the struggles of the world around them. Whether this "ivory tower" view of education was true in many places is questionable. It most certainly is not true of schools in America today. Almost every social problem affects school students—drug use, teenage pregnancies, broken families, and so on. In turn, these problems lead to a number of students coming to school who are unable or unwilling to learn, students who will drop out of school long before graduation. And in America today, people who lack a high school education have difficulty gaining employment at anything more than menial jobs.

Can music in the schools do anything to help students who are "at risk," who are likely to drop out of school? Yes and no. The problems of students at risk are often serious ones. Large and complex problems are not easily solved by any program, even ones that devote a lot of time and attention to the students. Music instruction in the schools is not set up and supported in a way that provides that degree or type of help. Therefore, the answer in many cases is "no."

In some cases, however, the answer is "yes." Directors of high school performing groups often have the same students for a number of years. In addition, they see them not only in classes and rehearsals but also in informal situations such as on trips or at athletic events. They probably know those students better than any other teacher in school. In fact, they sometimes know things about a student that even his or her parents don't know. For these reasons, music teachers can often influence students to a degree that other teachers can't. The music teacher is often a role model. The extended and informal contact with many students in performing groups makes music teachers far more influential as role models than other teachers in the middle and high schools.

The attraction of music groups for many at-risk students is something that educators have sensed for many years, but it has seldom been documented. When it has, the findings are impressive. A study conducted in Florida in 1990 uncovered the fact that over 70 percent of the secondary school principals interviewed could think of students who would have dropped out of school had it not been for the arts program (Florida Department of Education, 1990). Such evidence, as well as casual observation, points to the fact that music can be a powerful force in helping at-risk students. Equally true is the fact that music alone is not a panacea for the social ills of young people and society.

The challenge for music educators is to attract more at-risk students into music programs than is presently the case. If most high schools offer only intensive and demanding performing groups, then the music program will touch few of these students. Seldom can the afford the expense and commitment such groups demand. Therefore, music educators need to offer a wider variety of courses. A nonperformance course for the general students is a logical starting place for reaching more students (Hoffer, 1989). Other courses and music experiences should also be offered: ethnic music groups, guitar and similar instruments, rock band, and so on.

Many of these at-risk students are very active and knowledgeable in certain kinds of music. The problem is not that they dislike music. Rather, the situation often seems to be that the school music program as it presently exists in so many secondary schools doesn't meet their musical interests and needs. Should music teachers "lower their standards" to accommodate these students, or should music teachers require that at-risk students "shape up" and learn what's best for them? It's not a simple matter. Perhaps everyone should be more flexible and understanding than has often been true in the past.

TECHNOLOGY AND MUSIC EDUCATION

It is hardly news that technological advances have had an enormous impact on music and the way people experience music. Today they have much more music than people had in the past, and yet they probably pay less attention to it. Although it is much simpler to create music on an electronic keyboard with its preset sounds, few people seem interested in listening to new music. The ease of making music electronically has a tendency to discourage students from learning to sing or from making music on traditional instruments.

Music educators have had equally mixed feelings about technology. Some of them have flirted with, and generally discarded, radio, film, television, tachistoscopic readers, and other hardware. Other educators treat technological developments with fear and distrust, all the while wishing that such things would go away.

Well, they won't go away. In fact, they will become more important in the future than they are now. Why? What are the benefits of technology for music teachers? What can a computer do in teaching students that a book can't do? First, a computer with a good program in it can provide individualized instruction. If a student is not doing well on a topic, then the computer program can provide extra practice or instruction. While teachers generally must teach to the "middle of the class," computers help teachers meet the needs of both the slow and the able learners much better than in the past.

Second, a computer program can interact with the individual student. It can consider the responses of a student and offer comment about those responses or direct future study in certain directions.

Third, a computer and electronic keyboard can greatly reduce the technical barriers to participation in music. To render a musical idea in notation used to require quite a bit of musical knowledge. Not so today. All one need do is play the passage (with only one finger if necessary) to enter it into the computer. The computer program will then present what was played in notation (playing errors included!). Performance can be much simpler, too. With a flick of a switch one can transpose perfectly to any key, change tempo, or play entire chords with one finger. One could raise philosophical questions about being able to make music so easily and without the effort and commitment formerly required, but few people seem concerned about such matters.

Fourth, technology can save teachers time and effort. Computers can accomplish in a fraction of a second tasks that would take a person minutes or even hours to do.

What's the challenge to music educators with regard to technology? One challenge is to keep abreast of the new developments. Each year new equipment and programs appear. The *Music in Education* program by Yamaha mentioned in Chapter 8 is one such development. Whether teachers adopt it or not, they should know about it and make an informed judgment regarding its use.

Second, they need to take advantage of the opportunities that technology offers. For example, between 4 and 5 million electronic keyboards are sold in the United States each year. This fact means that music teachers in the elementary schools can assume that a majority of students in their classes have an electronic keyboard at home. Therefore, assignments or projects could be developed to make use of these instruments as an entrée to further music study.

Third, music educators must decide how best to use technology. In no sense are computers or compact disc players going to replace music teachers or books. Nor should electronic keyboards be a substitute for singing. The challenge, then, is to maintain a balance in the type of musical experiences the students are provided and to use technology appropriately.

The late twentieth and early twenty-first century is a great time to be a music educator. But that's always been true. Whatever else may be said about teaching music in the schools, it is not without its challenges and opportunities. And it's not without its rewards either.

Questions

1. Why is the quality of music instruction three-, four-, and five-year-old children receive important to all music educators?

2. Why is the limited education in music provided a majority of the students in middle schools a serious weakness in American music education?

3. What special challenges does the accurate assessment of learning in music present to music educators and assessment specialists?

4. Music is enjoyable and can be entertaining.
   a) In what ways is this fact helpful to music education?
   b) In what ways is this fact detrimental to music education?

5. What are some actions that music teachers can take to educate school administrators, school board members, parents, and the community about the purposes and the value of music in the school curriculum?

6. In what ways has fund-raising helped particular performing groups?

7. In what ways has fund-raising helped the total music program?

8. In what ways has fund-raising not been beneficial to school music programs?

9. Teaching some types of music in addition to traditional Western art and folk music is very desirable. What are some factors that challenge music educators in doing this?

10. Why are music teachers often more effective in helping at-risk students than other teachers?

11. Why can computers with good programs be more effective than books in teaching some (not all!) aspects of music?

Project Think of a musical work that might be performed in public by a school group. Answer the following questions about how that work could be used to educate an audience about music and music education.

1. What aspects of that work could the audience be informed about?

2. What aspects of what the students have learned from performing that work could the audience be informed about?

References Andress, B. (1989). *Promising practices: Prekindergarten music education.* Reston, VA: Music Educators National Conference.

The role of fine and performing art in high school dropout prevention (1990). Tallahassee, FL: Florida Department of Education.

Hoffer, C. R. (1989). A new frontier. *Music Educators Journal, 75*(7), 34.

The school music program: Description and standards (1986) (2nd ed.). Reston, VA: Music Educators National Conference.

Soundpost, 8.

CODA

As music educators face the 1990s and soon a new century, they can look back on a long and distinguished record of accomplishments by their profession. True, there are some storm clouds on the horizon (there always are) and problems that need to be faced (also always true). And music education is not all that it should be; not by a long sight! Perhaps one should look at music education somewhat as one might think about a dog walking on its hind legs. It's not that the animal walks imperfectly; rather, it's amazing that it can do it at all! Music education has achieved much under some pretty difficult circumstances.

If one were living in 1836 when Lowell Mason presented his proposal for music in the schools to the Boston Schools and were asked to predict the prospect of success for his idea, the chances are that it would be pronounced a nice but hopeless dream. To begin with, music and the arts do not have the practical benefits that most other subjects can claim; enriching the quality of people's lives does not carry the same immediate impact as a reason for including a subject in the school curriculum. Few people have ever appeared to understand the real value of an education in music for all students. Furthermore, music has seldom enjoyed the financial and administrative support it deserves. It has had to struggle for time in the school day and for other forms of academic recognition.

Often music education seems to be caught in the middle regarding what it should be. On the one hand, it has had to deal with what might be termed the "Joe Sixpacks" view on the part of the public and many school administrators that music is in the schools to provide entertainment, especially at athletic events. On the other hand, music education has had to fend off the criticisms of a few persons who consider themselves musically and/or intellectually superior and who want an elite type of music education program that would reach only a small number of students.

Fortunately, music education defied what logically should have been the fate of a quiet burial. Today it has achieved a scope and size that would astound Lowell Mason were he, by some warp of time, to return and observe school music programs. As long as music educators retain some of Mason's sense of vision and passion for music for all students, then there is no reason why music education should not continue to grow and improve in the future.

APPENDIX A

OFF-CAMPUS OBSERVATION FORM

Student's name:
Teacher observed:
School:
Date of observation:
Type of class observed:
Age or grade of students:

What appeared to be the objectives of the class?

How did the teacher try to achieve those objectives?

How did the students respond to the teaching procedures?

What methods of classroom control did you observe?

How well were the objectives of the class accomplished?

What did you particularly like about what the teacher did in teaching the class?

What would you try to do differently if you had been the teacher of the class?

Other information or thoughts:

APPENDIX B

The Music Code of Ethics

The Music Code of Ethics was originally adopted over thirty years ago, and it was slightly revised and reaffirmed in 1989 by the Music Educators National Conference, the American Federation of Musicians of the United States and Canada, the AFL-CIO, the American Association of School Administrators, the National Association of Elementary School Principals, and the National Association of Secondary School Principals.

Music educators and professional musicians alike are committed to the general acceptance of music as an essential factor in the social and cultural growth of our country. Music educators contributed to this end by fostering the study of music among children and by developing a greater interest in music.

This unanimity of purpose is further exemplified by the fact that a great many professional musicians are music educators and the fact that a great many music educators are, or have been, actively engaged in the field of professional performance.

The members of high school instrumental groups—orchestras and bands of all types, including stage bands—look to the professional organization for example and inspiration. The standards of quality acquired during the education of these students are of great importance when they become active patrons of music in later life. Through their influence on sponsors, employers, and program makers in demanding adequate musical performances, they have a beneficial effect upon the prestige and economic status of the professional musicians.

Since it is in the interest of the music educator to attract public attention to his attainments, not only for the main purpose of promoting the values of music education but also to enhance his position and subsequently his income, and since it is in the interest of the professional musician to create more opportunities for employment at increased remuneration, it is only natural that some incidents might occur in which the interest of the members of one or the other group might be infringed upon, either from lack of forethought or lack of ethical standards among individuals.

In order to establish a clear understanding as to the limitations of the fields of professional music and music education in the United States, the following statement of policy, adopted by the Music Educators National Conference and the American Federation of Musicians and approved by the American Association of School Administrators, the National Association of Elementary School Principals, and the National Association of Secondary School Principals, is recommended to those serving in their respective fields:

I. MUSIC EDUCATION

The field of music education, including the teaching of music and such demonstrations of music education as do not directly conflict with the interests of the professional musician, is the province of the music educator. It is the primary purpose of this document and the desire of all the parties signatory hereto that the professional musician shall have the fullest protection in his efforts to earn his living from the playing and rendition of music; to that end it is recognized and accepted that all music to be performed under this section of the "Code of Ethics" herein set forth is and shall be performed in connection with nonprofit, noncommercial, and noncompetitive enterprises. Under the heading of "Musical Education" the following are included:

1. *School functions* initiated by the schools as part of a school program, whether in a school building or other site.

2. *Community functions* organized in the interest of the schools strictly for educational purposes, such as those that might be originated by the parent and teachers association.

3. *School exhibits* prepared as a courtesy on the part of a school district for educational organizations or educational conventions being entertained in the district.

4. *Educational broadcasts* that have the purpose of demonstrating or illustrating pupils' achievements in music study or that represent the culmination of a period of study and rehearsal. Included in this category are local, state, regional, and national school music festivals and competitions held under the auspices of schools, colleges, and/or educational organizations on a nonprofit basis and broadcast to acquaint the public with the results of music instruction in the schools.

5. *Civic occasions* of local, state, or national patriotic interest, of sufficient breadth to enlist the sympathies and cooperation of all persons, such as those held by the American Legion and Veterans of Foreign Wars in connection with their Memorial Day services in the cemeteries. It is understood that affairs of this kind may be participated in only when such participation does not in the least usurp the rights and privileges of local professional musicians.

6. *Benefit performances* for local charities, such as the Red Cross and hospitals, when and where local professional musicians would likewise donate their services.

7. *Educational or civic services* that might be mutually agreed upon beforehand by the school authorities and official representative of the local professional musicians.

8. *Student or amateur recordings* for study purposes made in the classroom or in connection with contest, festival, or conference performances by students. Such recordings shall be limited to exclusive use by the students and their teachers and shall not be offered for general sale to the public through commercial outlets. This definition pertains only to the purpose and utilization of student or amateur recordings and not to matters concerned with copyright regulations. Compliance with copyright requirements applying to recordings or compositions not in the public domain is the responsibility of the school, college, or educational organization under whose auspices the recording is made.

II. ENTERTAINMENT

The field of entertainment is the province of the professional musician. Under this heading the following are included:

1. *Civic parades* (where professional marching bands exist), ceremonies, expositions, community concerts, and community-center activities; regattas; nonscholastic contests, festivals, athletic games, activities, or celebrations, and the like; and national, state, and county fairs (see section 1, paragraphs 2 and 5, of this document for further definition).

2. *Functions for the furtherance,* directly or indirectly, of any public or private enterprise; functions by chambers of commerce, boards of trade, and commercial clubs or associations.

3. *Any occasion that is partisan* or sectarian in character or purpose.

4. *Functions of clubs,* societies, and civic or fraternal organizations.

Statements that funds are not available for the employment of professional musicians; or that if the talents of amateur musical organizations cannot be had, other musicians cannot or will not be employed; or that the amateur musicians are to play without remuneration of any kind, are all immaterial.

This code is a continuing agreement that shall be reviewed regularly to make it responsive to changing conditions.

APPENDIX C

MENC POLICY STATEMENT ON FUND-RAISING

1. The basic curricular program of instruction in music in the schools should be funded from the school budget. As music is an essential component of the school curriculum, budgeted funding for music should include all staff, materials, equipment, and facilities necessary for a comprehensive basic music program as described in *The School Music Program: Description and Standards,* second edition.

2. Occasionally music instruction may be enriched by activities that are not normally funded from school budgets. Such activities include supplementary educational experiences and educational field trips that meet the guidelines of the Music Educators National Conference and the National Association of Secondary School Principals. Fund-raising for these purposes is justifiable if kept within reasonable limits.

3. If fund-raising is undertaken for the purpose of enriching the music education of students, it should:
   - require minimal time and effort on the part of students and teachers;
   - utilize no instructional time;
   - be appropriate for students;
   - adhere to the Code of Ethics of the American Federation of Musicians and the American Association of School Administrators.

4. The role of the music educator in any fund-raising activity should be:
   - as an advisor to the project;
   - to develop an overall plan, in cooperation with school administrators, parents, and students, for:
     - selecting an appropriate fund-raising activity;
     - implementing the project;
     - allocating the monies raised;
   - to delegate to a committee of parents and students the responsibility for record keeping, product handling, collection of funds and accounting;
   - to be knowledgeable about the financial aspects of the effort.

5. All fund-raising efforts should adhere to responsible standards of safety and well-being for the students. It is important that ethical and legal implications of the project be thoroughly understood in order to prevent jeopardizing the music teacher or program and to avoid situations which might result in litigation due to an accident or other misfortune.

[*Soundpost* 8(1) (Fall 1991), p. 15]

INDEX